THIS BOOK BELONGS TO

_____

START DATE

_____

SHE READS TRUTH

FOUNDERS

FOUNDER
Raechel Myers

CO-FOUNDER
Amanda Bible Williams

EXECUTIVE

CHIEF EXECUTIVE OFFICER
Ryan Myers

EDITORIAL

MANAGING EDITOR
Lindsey Jacobi, MDiv

PRODUCTION EDITOR
Hannah Little, MTS

ASSOCIATE EDITOR
Kayla De La Torre, MAT

COPY EDITOR
Becca Owens, MA

CREATIVE

SENIOR ART DIRECTOR
Annie Glover

DESIGN MANAGER
Kelsea Allen

DESIGNERS
Savannah Ault
Ashley Phillips

MARKETING

MARKETING LEAD
Kelsey Chapman

PRODUCT MARKETING MANAGER
Krista Squibb

CONTENT MARKETING STRATEGIST
Tameshia Williams, ThM

SOCIAL MEDIA SPECIALIST
Bella Ponce

OPERATIONS

OPERATIONS DIRECTOR
Allison Sutton

COMMUNITY ENGAGEMENT

COMMUNITY ENGAGEMENT MANAGER
Delaney Coleman

COMMUNITY ENGAGEMENT SPECIALISTS
Cait Baggerman
Katy McKnight

SHIPPING

SHIPPING MANAGER
Marian Welch

FULFILLMENT LEAD
Hannah Song

FULFILLMENT SPECIALISTS
Bonnie Nickander
Kelsey Simpson

SUBSCRIPTION INQUIRIES
orders@shereadstruth.com

CONTRIBUTORS

SPECIAL THANKS
John Greco, MDiv
Jessica Lamb, MA
Melanie Rainer, MATS
Kara Gause
Ellen Taylor
Emily Knapp Shambaugh
Davis DeLisi
Abbey Benson

SHE READS TRUTH™

© 2019, 2025 by She Reads Truth, LLC
All rights reserved. First edition 2019.
Second edition 2025.

All photography used by permission.

ISBN 978-1-962221-45-0

1 2 3 4 5 6 7 8 9 10

@SHEREADSTRUTH

Download the She Reads Truth app,
available for iOS and Android

Subscribe to the
She Reads Truth Podcast

This book was printed offset in Nashville, Tennessee, on 70# Lynx Opaque. Cover is Neenah Moonrock Smooth 120DTC with Infinity foil 90.

REVELATION

WORTHY IS THE LAMB

We are prompted to direct our gaze toward the throne of the only One who is worthy.

Lindsey

Lindsey Jacobi, MDiv
MANAGING EDITOR

et's just be honest right out of the gate, shall we? I mean, we're all friends here. When you think about reading the book of Revelation, you probably have a specific reaction. Be it fear, confusion, intrigue, elation—rarely is "neutral" the response to the grand finale of the Christian scriptures. For some, it brings out the instinct to solve a puzzle, with all the numbers and imagery appearing as pieces we want to try and fit together. For the more concrete thinkers, it might lead to frustration that Jesus's revelation to the apostle John wasn't more clear and straightforward. And for those of us who don't relish the adventure of uncertainty, the book of Revelation can simply feel daunting.

Personally, I find that no other book in Scripture is quite like Revelation, simultaneously bringing up questions and curiosity right alongside the deepest sensations of hope, trust, and assurance. There is a settling exhale that happens when you turn the final page. It doesn't come with a list of answers to all the questions that have been jotted in the margins. Instead, Revelation offers wisdom, insight, and hope for God's people so we know how to live with the end of the story in mind. This is not a fuzzy hope for the distant future; Revelation brings the kingdom of heaven into our everyday lives and asks us how we will respond.

I don't have many guarantees for your journey through this book. You might find the finish line of your study has tied up some bows for you. Or you might find you have a whole different set of questions than the ones you began with! You might even find the journey wasn't as scary as you thought it would be. But I do know this: It will be worth it.

I hope you take the opportunities we've provided in this Reading Guide to get down on the ground and explore a bit (check out the worksheets on pages 26, 40, 46, 78, and 103) without losing the forest for the trees. Remember where you're heading, and ask the Holy Spirit to give you glimpses of the greater story at hand. Beyond all of the imagery and poetry and prophecy—all part of Revelation's beautiful and intricate tapestry—we are prompted to direct our gaze toward the throne of the only One who is worthy. He is the same one who is the Firstborn of all creation. The same one born in human flesh. The same one who walked dusty roads with fickle disciples and made His way to die on a cross outside Jerusalem. The same one who rose from the dead and now sits at the right hand of the Father. This is Jesus—the Son of God, the Alpha and Omega, the Lion of Judah, the King of kings, and the Lord of lords. And He is coming again.

REVELATION: WORTHY IS THE LAMB

At She Reads Truth, we believe in pairing the inherently beautiful Word of God with the aesthetic beauty it deserves. Each of our resources is thoughtfully and artfully designed to highlight the beauty, goodness, and truth of Scripture in a way that reflects the themes of each curated reading plan.

The book of Revelation is extremely visual, from its detailed symbolism to its vivid descriptions of otherworldly places, creatures, and events.

One of the book's most glorious scenes is that of the new Jerusalem in chapter 21. In it, John describes the gemstones used to build the city walls—jewels including sapphire, emerald, amethyst, and jasper. While we don't know exactly what these gems will look like in the new Jerusalem, they were a fitting inspiration for the photography featured in this book (the names and corresponding numbers from Revelation 21 appear next to each photograph), offering our imaginations a glimpse of the glory to come.

The rich symbolism in Revelation inspired the minimalist icons you'll find alongside some of the book's more visual passages.

HOW TO USE THIS BOOK

She Reads Truth is a community of women dedicated to reading the Word of God every day. In this **Revelation** reading plan, we will read the book of Revelation, along with complementary passages of Scripture, to learn about how Jesus will one day return in all honor and glory to dwell with His people forever.

READ & REFLECT

Your **Revelation** book focuses primarily on Scripture, with added features to come alongside your time with God's Word.

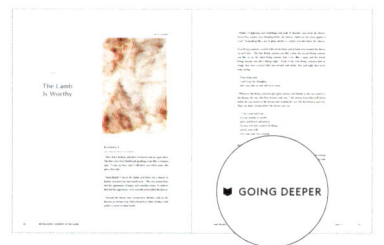

SCRIPTURE READING

Designed for a Monday start, this three-week reading plan presents the book of Revelation in daily readings, along with additional passages curated to show how the theme of the main reading can be found throughout Scripture.

🞂 *Additional passages are marked in your daily reading with the Going Deeper heading.*

WORKSHEETS

Select days feature an interactive worksheet to guide you as you read.

COMMUNITY & CONVERSATION

You can start reading this book at any time! If you want to join women from Stanford to Sweden as they read along with you, join us in the **Revelation** reading plan through our app or website and podcast.

📱 SHE READS TRUTH APP

Devotionals corresponding to each daily reading can be found in the **Revelation** reading plan in the She Reads Truth app. You can use the app to participate in community discussion and more.

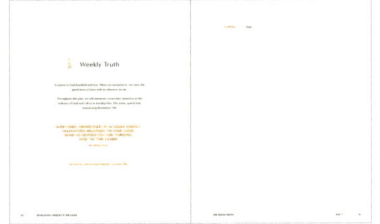

GRACE DAY

Use Saturdays to catch up on your reading, pray, and rest in the presence of the Lord.

WEEKLY TRUTH

Sundays are set aside for Scripture memorization.

See tips for memorizing Scripture on page 120.

EXTRAS

This book features additional tools to help you gain a deeper understanding of the text.

Find a complete list of extras on page 10.

 SHEREADSTRUTH.COM

The **Revelation** reading plan and devotionals will also be available at SheReadsTruth.com as the community reads each day. Invite your family, friends, and neighbors to read along with you!

 SHE READS TRUTH PODCAST

Subscribe to the She Reads Truth Podcast, and join our founders and their guests each week as they talk about the beauty, goodness, and truth they find in Scripture.

 Tune into episodes 303–305 for our ***Revelation*** *series.*

Table of Contents

Then I saw in the right hand of the one seated on the throne a scroll with writing on both sides, sealed with seven seals. I also saw a mighty angel proclaiming with a loud voice,

"Who is worthy to open the scroll and break its seals?"

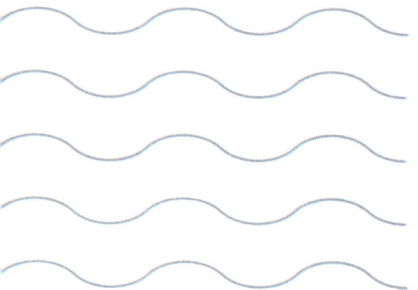

But no one in heaven or on earth or under the earth was able to open the scroll or even to look in it. I wept and wept because no one was found worthy to open the scroll or even to look in it.

REVELATION 5:1–4

KEY VERSE

Revelation 21:6

THEN HE SAID TO ME, "IT IS DONE! I AM THE ALPHA AND THE OMEGA, THE BEGINNING AND THE END. I WILL FREELY GIVE TO THE THIRSTY FROM THE SPRING OF THE WATER OF LIFE."

SHE READS REVELATION

On the Timeline

In light of the many possible dates for the writing of the book of Revelation, many scholars allow a window of thirty years, estimating it was written between the late-60s and the mid-90s of the first century AD. Substantial historical evidence shows that some of the churches mentioned in Revelation 2–3 were persecuted intensely by Nero in the late-60s. But others suggest the reference in Revelation 17:10 to seven kings, five of whom had fallen, supports a date in the mid-90s, during the reign of the Roman emperor Domitian who ruled from AD 81–96. Further evidence for this later date is the tradition that John the apostle was exiled to Patmos during a period of intense, localized persecution of Christians by emperor Domitian.

A Little Background

The author of Revelation is traditionally believed to be the apostle John, who wrote the Fourth Gospel and the three letters of 1, 2, and 3 John (Revelation 1:4, 9). The initial audience was a group of seven local churches in southwest Asia Minor (Revelation 1:11; 2–3). Some of these congregations were experiencing persecution (Revelation 2:9–10, 13), probably under Domitian. Others had doctrinal and practical problems (Revelation 2:6, 13–15, 20–23). Underlying these surface problems was the backdrop of unseen but powerful spiritual warfare (Revelation 2:10, 14, 24; 3:9).

Message & Purpose

The book of Revelation is named for the Greek word for apocalypse, *apokalypsis*. Revelation is a letter, prophecy, and an apocalyptic work (meaning it is a type of literature that describes, usually in big pictures and visual metaphors, God intervening in human history to accomplish judgmental and salvific work). The book of Revelation provides an almost complete overview of theology: the study of God and what we believe about Him. Much is said in this book about Christ, humanity and sin, the people of God, Satan and demons, and holy angels. Revelation also includes important material on God's power and the Trinity, plus aspects of the work of the Holy Spirit and the nature of Scripture.

More so than any other book in the Bible, the visions found in Revelation focus on events surrounding the full arrival of God's kingdom on earth. It also gives practical choices that believers and nonbelievers make in the course of their lives that contribute to how we will see God's kingdom on earth as we await Christ's second coming.

Give Thanks for the Book of Revelation

At its core, Revelation shows us the heart of God for His people and for all of creation—complete, uninterrupted unity with Him that is free from the suffering we endure now (Rv 21:3–4). These things were revealed and written so that all could know God's will for those He loves. Though complex at times, Revelation is a testament to God's desire to restore all things and the ways He gives of Himself in order to accomplish this purpose.

Reminders for Reading the Book of Revelation

1 — Revelation employs numerology, a style of writing that communicates meaning through significant numbers, and symbolism, using images to communicate larger ideas. These methods of writing help us connect with God even as we encounter unfamiliar or confusing passages.

2 — Being a work of apocalyptic literature, Revelation contains truth for the past, present, and the future. The events detailed are not always linear, as the book contains flashbacks and flashforwards and includes cyclical, repeated patterns of judgment and salvation.

3 — While Revelation's events and timeline are largely a mystery, what we learn about God's character and will in this book of the Bible is consistent with who He is throughout Scripture.

DAY 1

The Living One

Revelation 1

PROLOGUE

[1] The revelation of Jesus Christ that God gave him to show his servants what must soon take place. He made it known by sending his angel to his servant John, [2] who testified to the word of God and to the testimony of Jesus Christ, whatever he saw. [3] Blessed is the one who reads aloud the words of this prophecy, and blessed are those who hear the words of this prophecy and keep what is written in it, because the time is near.

[4] John: To the seven churches in Asia. Grace and peace to you from the one who is, who was, and who is to come, and from the seven spirits before his throne, [5] and from Jesus Christ, the faithful witness, the firstborn from the dead and the ruler of the kings of the earth.

To him who loves us and has set us free from our sins by his blood, ⁶ and made us a kingdom, priests to his God and Father—to him be glory and dominion forever and ever. Amen.

⁷ Look, he is coming with the clouds,
and every eye will see him,
even those who pierced him.
And all the tribes of the earth
will mourn over him.
So it is to be. Amen.

⁸ "I AM THE ALPHA AND THE OMEGA,"
SAYS THE LORD GOD, "THE ONE WHO IS,
WHO WAS, AND WHO IS TO COME,
THE ALMIGHTY."

JOHN'S VISION OF THE RISEN LORD

⁹ I, John, your brother and partner in the affliction, kingdom, and endurance that are in Jesus, was on the island called Patmos because of the word of God and the testimony of Jesus. ¹⁰ I was in the Spirit on the Lord's day, and I heard a loud voice behind me like a trumpet ¹¹ saying, "Write on a scroll what you see and send it to the seven churches: Ephesus, Smyrna, Pergamum, Thyatira, Sardis, Philadelphia, and Laodicea."

¹² Then I turned to see whose voice it was that spoke to me. When I turned I saw seven golden lampstands, ¹³ and among the lampstands was one like the Son of Man, dressed in a robe and with a golden sash wrapped around his chest. ¹⁴ The hair of his head was white as wool—white as snow—and his eyes like a fiery flame. ¹⁵ His feet were like fine bronze as it is fired in a furnace, and his voice like the sound of cascading waters. ¹⁶ He had seven stars in his right hand; a sharp double-edged sword came from his mouth, and his face was shining like the sun at full strength.

¹⁷ When I saw him, I fell at his feet like a dead man. He laid his right hand on me and said, "Don't be afraid. I am the First and the Last, ¹⁸ and the Living One. I was dead, but look—I am alive forever and ever, and I hold the keys of death and Hades. ¹⁹ Therefore write what you have seen, what is, and what will take place after this. ²⁰ The mystery of the seven stars you saw in my right hand and of the seven golden lampstands is this: The seven stars are the angels of the seven churches, and the seven lampstands are the seven churches."

1 Corinthians 15:54–57

54 When this corruptible body is clothed with incorruptibility, and this mortal body is clothed with immortality, then the saying that is written will take place:

Death has been swallowed up in victory.
55 Where, death, is your victory?
Where, death, is your sting?

56 The sting of death is sin, and the power of sin is the law. 57 But thanks be to God, who gives us the victory through our Lord Jesus Christ!

1 Thessalonians 4:13–17

THE COMFORT OF CHRIST'S COMING

13 We do not want you to be uninformed, brothers and sisters, concerning those who are asleep, so that you will not grieve like the rest, who have no hope. 14 For if we believe that Jesus died and rose again, in the same way, through Jesus, God will bring with him those who have fallen asleep. 15 For we say this to you by a word from the Lord: We who are still alive at the Lord's coming will certainly not precede those who have fallen asleep. 16 For the Lord himself will descend from heaven with a shout, with the archangel's voice, and with the trumpet of God, and the dead in Christ will rise first. 17 Then we who are still alive, who are left, will be caught up together with them in the clouds to meet the Lord in the air, and so we will always be with the Lord.

	Date
NOTES	

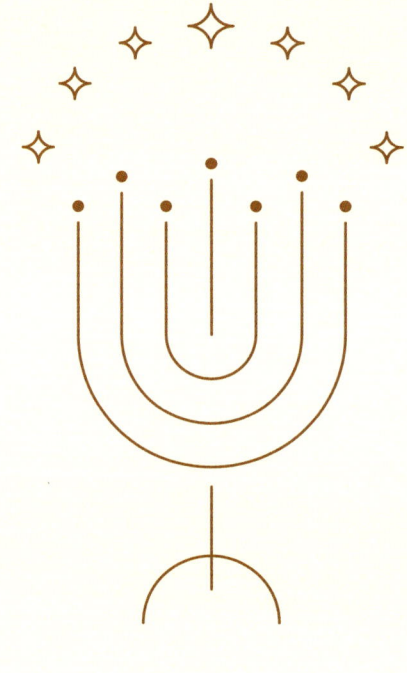

MAP

The Seven Churches

"The mystery of the seven stars you saw in my right hand and of the seven golden lampstands is this: The seven stars are the angels of the seven churches, and the seven lampstands are the seven churches."

REVELATION 1:20

MARMARA SEA

Asia
Minor

AEGEAN SEA

● Pergamum

● Thyatira

● Smyrna

● Sardis

● Philadelphia

● Ephesus

● Laodicea

PATMOS

N
W E
S

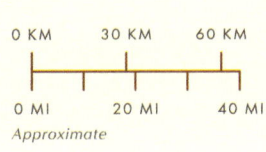

0 KM   30 KM   60 KM

0 MI   20 MI   40 MI
Approximate

MEDITERRANEAN SEA

The Seven Churches

Use the worksheet found on page 26 to take notes as you read.

Revelation 2

THE LETTERS TO THE SEVEN CHURCHES

THE LETTER TO EPHESUS

¹ "Write to the angel of the church in Ephesus: Thus says the one who holds the seven stars in his right hand and who walks among the seven golden lampstands: ² I know your works, your labor, and your endurance, and that you cannot tolerate evil people. You have tested those who call themselves apostles and are not, and you have found them to be liars. ³ I know that you have persevered and endured hardships for the sake of my name, and you have not grown weary. ⁴ But I have this against you: You have abandoned the love you had at first. ⁵ Remember then how far you have fallen; repent, and do the works you did at first. Otherwise, I will come to you and remove your lampstand from its place, unless you repent. ⁶ Yet you do have this: You hate the practices of the Nicolaitans, which I also hate.

⁷ "Let anyone who has ears to hear listen to what the Spirit says to the churches. To the one who conquers, I will give the right to eat from the tree of life, which is in the paradise of God.

THE LETTER TO SMYRNA

⁸ "Write to the angel of the church in Smyrna: Thus says the First and the Last, the one who was dead and came to life:

⁹ I know your affliction and poverty, but you are rich. I know the slander of those who say they are Jews and are not, but are a synagogue of Satan. ¹⁰ Don't be afraid of what you are about to suffer. Look, the devil is about to throw some of you into prison to test you, and you will experience affliction for ten days. Be faithful to the point of death, and I will give you the crown of life.

¹¹ "Let anyone who has ears to hear listen to what the Spirit says to the churches. The one who conquers will never be harmed by the second death.

THE LETTER TO PERGAMUM

¹² "Write to the angel of the church in Pergamum: Thus says the one who has the sharp, double-edged sword: ¹³ I know where you live—where Satan's throne is. Yet you are holding on to my name and did not deny your faith in me, even in the days of Antipas, my faithful witness who was put to death among you, where Satan lives. ¹⁴ But I have a few things against you. You have some there who hold to the teaching of Balaam, who taught Balak to place a stumbling block in front of the Israelites: to eat meat sacrificed to idols and to commit sexual immorality. ¹⁵ In the same way, you also have those who hold to the teaching of the Nicolaitans.

"LET ANYONE WHO HAS EARS TO HEAR LISTEN TO WHAT THE SPIRIT SAYS TO THE CHURCHES."

Revelation 2:29

16 So repent! Otherwise, I will come to you quickly and fight against them with the sword of my mouth.

17 "Let anyone who has ears to hear listen to what the Spirit says to the churches. To the one who conquers, I will give some of the hidden manna. I will also give him a white stone, and on the stone a new name is inscribed that no one knows except the one who receives it.

THE LETTER TO THYATIRA

18 "Write to the angel of the church in Thyatira: Thus says the Son of God, the one whose eyes are like a fiery flame and whose feet are like fine bronze: 19 I know your works—your love, faithfulness, service, and endurance. I know that your last works are greater than the first. 20 But I have this against you: You tolerate the woman Jezebel, who calls herself a prophetess and teaches and deceives my servants to commit sexual immorality and to eat meat sacrificed to idols. 21 I gave her time to repent, but she does not want to repent of her sexual immorality. 22 Look, I will throw her into a sickbed and those who commit adultery with her into great affliction. Unless they repent of her works, 23 I will strike her children dead. Then all the churches will know that I am the one who examines minds and hearts, and I will give to each of you according to your works. 24 I say to the rest of you in Thyatira, who do not hold this teaching, who haven't known "the so-called secrets of Satan" —as they say—I am not putting any other burden on you. 25 Only hold on to what you have until I come. 26 The one who conquers and who keeps my works to the end: I will give him authority over the nations—

27 and he will rule them with an iron scepter;
he will shatter them like pottery —

28 just as I have received this from my Father. I will also give him the morning star.

29 "Let anyone who has ears to hear listen to what the Spirit says to the churches."

Revelation 3

THE LETTER TO SARDIS

[1] "Write to the angel of the church in Sardis: Thus says the one who has the seven spirits of God and the seven stars: I know your works; you have a reputation for being alive, but you are dead. [2] Be alert and strengthen what remains, which is about to die, for I have not found your works complete before my God. [3] Remember, then, what you have received and heard; keep it, and repent. If you are not alert, I will come like a thief, and you have no idea at what hour I will come upon you. [4] But you have a few people in Sardis who have not defiled their clothes, and they will walk with me in white, because they are worthy.

[5] "In the same way, the one who conquers will be dressed in white clothes, and I will never erase his name from the book of life but will acknowledge his name before my Father and before his angels.

[6] "Let anyone who has ears to hear listen to what the Spirit says to the churches.

THE LETTER TO PHILADELPHIA

[7] "Write to the angel of the church in Philadelphia: Thus says the Holy One, the true one, the one who has the key of David, who opens and no one will close, and who closes and no one opens: [8] I know your works. Look, I have placed before you an open door that no one can close because you have but little power; yet you have kept my word and have not denied my name. [9] Note this: I will make those from the synagogue of Satan, who claim to be Jews and are not, but are lying—I will make them come and bow down at your feet, and they will know that I have loved you. [10] Because you have kept my command to endure, I will also keep you from the hour of testing that is going to come on the whole world to test those who live on the earth. [11] I am coming soon. Hold on to what you have, so that no one takes your crown.

[12] "The one who conquers I will make a pillar in the temple of my God, and he will never go out again. I will write on him the name of my God and the name of the city of my God—the new Jerusalem, which comes down out of heaven from my God—and my new name.

[13] "Let anyone who has ears to hear listen to what the Spirit says to the churches.

THE LETTER TO LAODICEA

[14] "Write to the angel of the church in Laodicea: Thus says the Amen, the faithful and true witness, the originator of God's creation: [15] I know your works, that you are neither cold nor hot. I wish that you were cold or hot. [16] So, because you are lukewarm, and neither hot nor cold, I am going to vomit you out of my mouth. [17] For you say, 'I'm rich; I have become wealthy and need nothing,' and you don't realize that you are wretched, pitiful, poor, blind, and naked. [18] I advise you to buy from me gold refined in the fire so that you may be rich, white clothes so that you may be dressed and your shameful nakedness not be exposed, and ointment to spread on your eyes so that you may see. [19] As many as I love, I rebuke and discipline. So be zealous and repent. [20] See! I stand at the door and knock. If anyone hears my voice and opens the door, I will come in to him and eat with him, and he with me.

[21] "To the one who conquers I will give the right to sit with me on my throne, just as I also conquered and sat down with my Father on his throne.

[22] "Let anyone who has ears to hear listen to what the Spirit says to the churches."

🔖 GOING DEEPER

Matthew 22:34–39

THE PRIMARY COMMANDS

[34] When the Pharisees heard that he had silenced the Sadducees, they came together. [35] And one of them, an expert in the law, asked a question to test him: [36] "Teacher, which command in the law is the greatest?"

[37] He said to him, "Love the Lord your God with all your heart, with all your soul, and with all your mind. [38] This is the greatest and most important command. [39] The second is like it: Love your neighbor as yourself."

NOTES	Date

The Seven Churches

| Complete this chart as you read the letters to the seven churches in chapters 2 and 3.

	EPHESUS Rv 2:1–7	SMYRNA Rv 2:8–11	PERGAMUM Rv 2:12–17
Description of Christ	Holds seven stars in His right hand Walks among seven golden lampstands		
Affirmation	Works, labor, endurance Could not tolerate evil people Tested false apostles Persevered and endured hardships Hated practices of Nicolaitans		
Rebuke	Abandoned the love they first had	*No rebuke*	
Promise	The one who conquers will be given the right to eat from the tree of life.		

THYATIRA

Rv 2:18–29

SARDIS

Rv 3:1–6

PHILADELPHIA

Rv 3:7–13

LAODICEA

Rv 3:14–22

No affirmation

No rebuke

No. 6: Carnelian

DAY 3

The Lamb Is Worthy

Revelation 4

THE THRONE ROOM OF HEAVEN

¹ After this I looked, and there in heaven was an open door. The first voice that I had heard speaking to me like a trumpet said, "Come up here, and I will show you what must take place after this."

² Immediately I was in the Spirit, and there was a throne in heaven and someone was seated on it. ³ The one seated there had the appearance of jasper and carnelian stone. A rainbow that had the appearance of an emerald surrounded the throne.

⁴ Around the throne were twenty-four thrones, and on the thrones sat twenty-four elders dressed in white clothes, with golden crowns on their heads.

⁵ Flashes of lightning and rumblings and peals of thunder came from the throne. Seven fiery torches were burning before the throne, which are the seven spirits of God. ⁶ Something like a sea of glass, similar to crystal, was also before the throne.

Four living creatures covered with eyes in front and in back were around the throne on each side. ⁷ The first living creature was like a lion; the second living creature was like an ox; the third living creature had a face like a man; and the fourth living creature was like a flying eagle. ⁸ Each of the four living creatures had six wings; they were covered with eyes around and inside. Day and night they never stop, saying,

> Holy, holy, holy,
> Lord God, the Almighty,
> who was, who is, and who is to come.

⁹ Whenever the living creatures give glory, honor, and thanks to the one seated on the throne, the one who lives forever and ever, ¹⁰ the twenty-four elders fall down before the one seated on the throne and worship the one who lives forever and ever. They cast their crowns before the throne and say,

> ¹¹ Our Lord and God,
> you are worthy to receive
> glory and honor and power,
> because you have created all things,
> and by your will
> they exist and were created.

Revelation 5

THE LAMB TAKES THE SCROLL

¹ Then I saw in the right hand of the one seated on the throne a scroll with writing on both sides, sealed with seven seals. ² I also saw a mighty angel proclaiming with a loud voice,

"WHO IS WORTHY TO OPEN THE SCROLL AND BREAK ITS SEALS?"

³ But no one in heaven or on earth or under the earth was able to open the scroll or even to look in it. ⁴ I wept and wept because no one was found worthy to open the scroll or even to look in it. ⁵ Then one of the elders said to me, "Do not weep. Look, the Lion from the tribe of Judah, the Root of David, has conquered so that he is able to open the scroll and its seven seals."

⁶ Then I saw one like a slaughtered lamb standing in the midst of the throne and the four living creatures and among the elders. He had seven horns and seven eyes,

which are the seven spirits of God sent into all the earth. [7] He went and took the scroll out of the right hand of the one seated on the throne.

THE LAMB IS WORTHY

[8] When he took the scroll, the four living creatures and the twenty-four elders fell down before the Lamb. Each one had a harp and golden bowls filled with incense, which are the prayers of the saints. [9] And they sang a new song:

> You are worthy to take the scroll
> and to open its seals,
> because you were slaughtered,
> and you purchased people
> for God by your blood
> from every tribe and language
> and people and nation.
> [10] You made them a kingdom
> and priests to our God,
> and they will reign on the earth.

[11] Then I looked and heard the voice of many angels around the throne, and also of the living creatures and of the elders. Their number was countless thousands, plus thousands of thousands. [12] They said with a loud voice,

> Worthy is the Lamb who was slaughtered
> to receive power and riches
> and wisdom and strength
> and honor and glory and blessing!

[13] I heard every creature in heaven, on earth, under the earth, on the sea, and everything in them say,

> Blessing and honor and glory and power
> be to the one seated on the throne,
> and to the Lamb, forever and ever!

[14] The four living creatures said, "Amen," and the elders fell down and worshiped.

◗ GOING DEEPER

Isaiah 6:1–6

ISAIAH'S CALL AND MISSION

[1] In the year that King Uzziah died, I saw the Lord seated on a high and lofty throne, and the hem of his robe filled the temple. [2] Seraphim were standing above him; they each had six wings: with two they covered their faces, with two they covered their feet, and with two they flew. [3] And one called to another:

> Holy, holy, holy is the LORD of Armies;
> his glory fills the whole earth.

[4] The foundations of the doorways shook at the sound of their voices, and the temple was filled with smoke.

[5] Then I said:

> Woe is me for I am ruined
> because I am a man of unclean lips
> and live among a people of unclean lips,
> and because my eyes have seen the King,
> the LORD of Armies.

[6] Then one of the seraphim flew to me, and in his hand was a glowing coal that he had taken from the altar with tongs.

Ezekiel 1:26–28

[26] Something like a throne with the appearance of lapis lazuli was above the expanse over their heads. On the throne, high above, was someone who looked like a human. [27] From what seemed to be his waist up, I saw a gleam like amber, with what looked like fire enclosing it all around. From what seemed to be his waist down, I also saw what looked like fire. There was a brilliant light all around him. [28] The appearance of the brilliant light all around was like that of a rainbow in a cloud on a rainy day. This was the appearance of the likeness of the LORD's glory. When I saw it, I fell facedown and heard a voice speaking.

NOTES	Date

DESCRIPTIONS OF

Jesus in Revelation

In the Gospels, Jesus's nature is revealed: He is
fully human and fully God. Yet many people who
encountered Him on earth only saw His humanity as
He walked, talked, and lived as a man. The picture of
Jesus in Revelation is one of unimaginable glory and
splendor, emphasizing His divinity. The following pages
include a collection of descriptions of Jesus in the book
of Revelation, with references to where some of these
descriptions appear elsewhere in the Bible.

HE IS THE ONE WHO IS, AND WAS, AND IS TO COME.

Rv 1:4, 8; 4:8; 11:17; 16:5

HE IS THE FAITHFUL WITNESS.

Rv 1:5; 3:14 | *See Ps 89:37*

HE IS THE FIRSTBORN FROM THE DEAD.

Rv 1:5 | *See Ac 26:23; Col 1:18*

HE IS THE RULER OF THE KINGS OF THE EARTH.

Rv 1:5 | *See Ps 89:27*

HE IS THE ALPHA AND OMEGA.

Rv 1:8; 21:6; 22:13

HIS VOICE IS LOUD LIKE A TRUMPET.

Rv 1:10

HE IS THE SON OF MAN.

Rv 1:12–13; 14:14 | *See Dn 7:13; Mt 9:6; 10:23; 11:19*

HE IS DRESSED IN A ROBE WITH A GOLDEN SASH.

Rv 1:13 | *See Dn 10:5*

HIS HAIR IS WHITE AS WOOL AND SNOW.

Rv 1:14 | *See Dn 7:9*

HIS EYES ARE LIKE A FIERY FLAME.

Rv 1:14; 2:18; 19:12 | *See Dn 10:6*

HIS FEET ARE LIKE FINE BRONZE.

Rv 1:15; 2:18 | See Dn 10:6

HIS VOICE IS LIKE
CASCADING WATERS.

Rv 1:15 | See Ezk 1:24; 43:2

HE HOLDS SEVEN STARS IN HIS
RIGHT HAND.

Rv 1:16; 2:1; 3:1

HE HAS A SHARP,
DOUBLE-EDGED SWORD
COMING FROM HIS MOUTH.

Rv 1:16; 2:16; 19:15

HIS FACE SHINES LIKE THE SUN
AT FULL STRENGTH.

Rv 1:16 | See Mt 17:2

HE IS THE FIRST AND THE LAST.

Rv 1:17; 2:8; 22:13 | See Is 41:4; 44:6; 48:12

HE IS THE LIVING ONE.

Rv 1:18 | See Mt 16:16

HE IS ALIVE FOREVER AND EVER.

Rv 1:18 | See Rm 6:9

HE HOLDS THE KEYS OF DEATH
AND HADES.

Rv 1:18 | See Mt 16:18–19

HE HAS THE KEY OF DAVID.

Rv 3:7 | See Is 22:22

HE IS THE AMEN.

Rv 3:14

HE IS THE ORIGINATOR
OF GOD'S CREATION.

Rv 3:14 | See Jn 1:3

HE IS THE LION FROM THE
TRIBE OF JUDAH.

Rv 5:5 | See Gn 49:9–10

HE IS THE ROOT OF DAVID.

Rv 5:5; 22:16 | See Is 11:10; Rm 15:12

HE IS LIKE A SLAUGHTERED
LAMB WITH SEVEN HORNS
AND SEVEN EYES.

Rv 5:6

HE IS THE LAMB.

Rv 7:17; 14:1; 17:14; 21:22 | *See Jn 1:29, 36; 1Pt 1:19*

HE SHEPHERDS HIS PEOPLE.

Rv 7:17 | *See Ps 23:1; Jn 10:11–18*

HE RULES WITH AN IRON ROD.

Rv 12:5; 19:15 | *See Ps 2:9*

HE IS SEATED ON A CLOUD, WITH A GOLDEN CROWN AND A SHARP SICKLE.

Rv 14:14 | *See Dn 7:13; Lk 21:27*

HE TRAMPLES THE WINEPRESS OF THE FIERCE ANGER OF GOD.

Rv 14:14–20; 19:15 | *See Is 63:3*

HE IS LORD OF LORDS AND KING OF KINGS.

Rv 17:14; 19:16 | *See Dt 10:17; Ps 136:3; Dn 2:47; 1Tm 6:15*

HE HAS MANY CROWNS ON HIS HEAD.

Rv 19:12

HE HAS A NAME NO ONE KNOWS EXCEPT HIMSELF.

Rv 19:12

HE WEARS A ROBE DIPPED IN BLOOD.

Rv 19:13 | *See Is 63:1–3*

HE IS THE WORD OF GOD.

Rv 19:13 | *See Jn 1:1*

HE IS THE BEGINNING AND THE END.

Rv 21:6; 22:13

HE IS THE TEMPLE IN THE NEW JERUSALEM.

Rv 21:22

HE IS THE LAMP OF THE NEW JERUSALEM.

Rv 21:23 | *See Is 24:23; 60:19–20*

HE IS THE BRIGHT MORNING STAR.

Rv 22:16 | *See Nm 24:17*

DAY 4

How Long, O Lord?

Use the worksheet found on page 40 to take notes as you read.

Revelation 6

THE FIRST SEAL ON THE SCROLL

[1] Then I saw the Lamb open one of the seven seals, and I heard one of the four living creatures say with a voice like thunder, "Come!" [2] I looked, and there was a white horse. Its rider held a bow; a crown was given to him, and he went out as a conqueror in order to conquer.

THE SECOND SEAL

[3] When he opened the second seal, I heard the second living creature say, "Come!" [4] Then another horse went out, a fiery red one, and its rider was allowed to take peace from the earth, so that people would slaughter one another. And a large sword was given to him.

5 When he opened the third seal, I heard the third living creature say, "Come!" And I looked, and there was a black horse. Its rider held a set of scales in his hand. 6 Then I heard something like a voice among the four living creatures say, "A quart of wheat for a denarius, and three quarts of barley for a denarius, but do not harm the oil and the wine."

THE FOURTH SEAL

7 When he opened the fourth seal, I heard the voice of the fourth living creature say, "Come!" 8 And I looked, and there was a pale green horse. Its rider was named Death, and Hades was following after him. They were given authority over a fourth of the earth, to kill by the sword, by famine, by plague, and by the wild animals of the earth.

THE FIFTH SEAL

9 When he opened the fifth seal, I saw under the altar the souls of those who had been slaughtered because of the word of God and the testimony they had given. 10 They cried out with a loud voice, "Lord, the one who is holy and true, how long until you judge those who live on the earth and avenge our blood?" 11 So they were each given a white robe, and they were told to rest a little while longer until the number would be completed of their fellow servants and their brothers and sisters, who were going to be killed just as they had been.

THE SIXTH SEAL

12 Then I saw him open the sixth seal. A violent earthquake occurred; the sun turned black like sackcloth made of hair; the entire moon became like blood; 13 the stars of heaven fell to the earth as a fig tree drops its unripe figs when shaken by a high wind; 14 the sky was split apart like a scroll being rolled up; and every mountain and island was moved from its place.

15 Then the kings of the earth, the nobles, the generals, the rich, the powerful, and every slave and free person hid in the caves and among the rocks of the mountains. 16 And they said to the mountains and to the rocks, "Fall on us and hide us from the face of the one seated on the throne and from the wrath of the Lamb, 17 because the great day of their wrath has come! And who is able to stand?"

Revelation 7

THE SEALED OF ISRAEL

1 After this I saw four angels standing at the four corners of the earth, restraining the four winds of the earth so that no wind could blow on the earth or on the sea or on any tree. 2 Then I saw another angel rising up from the east, who had the seal of the living God. He cried out in a loud voice to the four angels who were allowed to harm the earth and the sea, 3 "Don't harm the earth or the sea or the trees until we seal the servants of our God on their foreheads." 4 And I heard the number of the sealed:

144,000 sealed from every tribe of the Israelites:
5 12,000 sealed from the tribe of Judah,
12,000 from the tribe of Reuben,
12,000 from the tribe of Gad,
6 12,000 from the tribe of Asher,
12,000 from the tribe of Naphtali,
12,000 from the tribe of Manasseh,
7 12,000 from the tribe of Simeon,
12,000 from the tribe of Levi,
12,000 from the tribe of Issachar,
8 12,000 from the tribe of Zebulun,
12,000 from the tribe of Joseph,
12,000 sealed from the tribe of Benjamin.

A MULTITUDE FROM THE GREAT TRIBULATION

9 After this I looked, and there was a vast multitude from every nation, tribe, people, and language, which no one could number, standing before the throne and before the Lamb. They were clothed in white robes with palm branches in their hands. 10 And they cried out in a loud voice:

Salvation belongs to our God,
who is seated on the throne,
and to the Lamb!

11 All the angels stood around the throne, and along with the elders and the four living creatures they fell facedown before the throne and worshiped God, 12 saying,

Amen! Blessing and glory and wisdom
and thanksgiving and honor

and power and strength
be to our God forever and ever. Amen.

¹³ Then one of the elders asked me, "Who are these people in white robes, and where did they come from?"

¹⁴ I said to him, "Sir, you know."

Then he told me: These are the ones coming out of the great tribulation. They washed their robes and made them white in the blood of the Lamb.

¹⁵ For this reason they are before the throne of God,
and they serve him day and night in his temple.
The one seated on the throne will shelter them:
¹⁶ They will no longer hunger;
they will no longer thirst;
the sun will no longer strike them,
nor will any scorching heat.
¹⁷ For the Lamb who is at the center of the throne
will shepherd them;
he will guide them to springs of the waters of life,
and God will wipe away every tear from their eyes.

❤ GOING DEEPER

Psalm 13

A PLEA FOR DELIVERANCE

For the choir director. A psalm of David.

¹ How long, LORD? Will you forget me forever?
How long will you hide your face from me?

² How long will I store up anxious concerns within me,
agony in my mind every day?
How long will my enemy dominate me?

³ Consider me and answer, LORD my God.
Restore brightness to my eyes;
otherwise, I will sleep in death.
⁴ My enemy will say, "I have triumphed over him,"
and my foes will rejoice because I am shaken.

⁵ BUT I HAVE TRUSTED IN
YOUR FAITHFUL LOVE;
MY HEART WILL REJOICE IN
YOUR DELIVERANCE.

⁶ I will sing to the LORD
because he has treated me generously.

Ephesians 1:11–14

¹¹ In him we have also received an inheritance, because we were predestined according to the plan of the one who works out everything in agreement with the purpose of his will, ¹² so that we who had already put our hope in Christ might bring praise to his glory.

¹³ In him you also were sealed with the promised Holy Spirit when you heard the word of truth, the gospel of your salvation, and when you believed. ¹⁴ The Holy Spirit is the down payment of our inheritance, until the redemption of the possession, to the praise of his glory.

The Seven Seals

Use the references provided to fill in what happens when each scroll is opened in Revelation 6 and 8.

1 Rv 6:1–2	**2** Rv 6:3–4	**3** Rv 6:5–6
One of the living creatures said "Come!" with a voice like thunder. A white horse appeared. The rider held a bow, was given a crown, and went out to conquer.		

| **4** | Rv 6:7–8 | | **5** | Rv 6:9–11 | | **6** | Rv 6:12–17 | | **7** | Rv 8:1–5 |

DAY 5

The Trumpets

Use the worksheets found on pages 40 and 46 to take notes as you read.

Revelation 8

THE SEVENTH SEAL

¹ When he opened the seventh seal, there was silence in heaven for about half an hour. ² Then I saw the seven angels who stand in the presence of God; seven trumpets were given to them. ³ Another angel, with a golden incense burner, came and stood at the altar. He was given a large amount of incense to offer with the prayers of all the saints on the golden altar in front of the throne. ⁴ The smoke of the incense, with the prayers of the saints, went up in the presence of God from the angel's hand. ⁵ The angel took the incense burner, filled it with fire from the altar, and hurled it to the earth; there were peals of thunder, rumblings, flashes of lightning, and an earthquake.

THE SEVEN TRUMPETS

⁶ And the seven angels who had the seven trumpets prepared to blow them.

THE FIRST TRUMPET

⁷ The first angel blew his trumpet, and hail and fire, mixed with blood, were hurled to the earth. So a third of the earth was burned up, a third of the trees were burned up, and all the green grass was burned up.

THE SECOND TRUMPET

⁸ The second angel blew his trumpet, and something like a great mountain ablaze with fire was hurled into the sea. So a third of the sea became blood, ⁹ a third of the living creatures in the sea died, and a third of the ships were destroyed.

THE THIRD TRUMPET

¹⁰ The third angel blew his trumpet, and a great star, blazing like a torch, fell from heaven. It fell on a third of the rivers and springs of water. ¹¹ The name of the star is Wormwood, and a third of the waters became wormwood. So, many of the people died from the waters, because they had been made bitter.

THE FOURTH TRUMPET

¹² The fourth angel blew his trumpet, and a third of the sun was struck, a third of the moon, and a third of the stars, so that a third of them were darkened. A third of the day was without light and also a third of the night.

¹³ I looked and heard an eagle flying high overhead, crying out in a loud voice, "Woe! Woe! Woe to those who live on the earth, because of the remaining trumpet blasts that the three angels are about to sound!"

THE SMOKE OF THE INCENSE, WITH THE PRAYERS OF THE SAINTS, WENT UP IN THE PRESENCE OF GOD FROM THE ANGEL'S HAND.

Revelation 8:4

Revelation 9

THE FIFTH TRUMPET

[1] The fifth angel blew his trumpet, and I saw a star that had fallen from heaven to earth. The key for the shaft to the abyss was given to him. [2] He opened the shaft to the abyss, and smoke came up out of the shaft like smoke from a great furnace so that the sun and the air were darkened by the smoke from the shaft. [3] Then locusts came out of the smoke on to the earth, and power was given to them like the power that scorpions have on the earth. [4] They were told not to harm the grass of the earth, or any green plant, or any tree, but only those people who do not have God's seal on their foreheads. [5] They were not permitted to kill them but were to torment them for five months; their torment is like the torment caused by a scorpion when it stings someone. [6] In those days people will seek death and will not find it; they will long to die, but death will flee from them.

[7] The appearance of the locusts was like horses prepared for battle. Something like golden crowns was on their heads; their faces were like human faces; [8] they had hair like women's hair; their teeth were like lions' teeth; [9] they had chests like iron breastplates; the sound of their wings was like the sound of many chariots with horses rushing into battle; [10] and they had tails with stingers like scorpions, so that with their tails they had the power to harm people for five months. [11] They had as their king the angel of the abyss; his name in Hebrew is Abaddon, and in Greek he has the name Apollyon.

[12] The first woe has passed. There are still two more woes to come after this.

THE SIXTH TRUMPET

[13] The sixth angel blew his trumpet. From the four horns of the golden altar that is before God, I heard a voice [14] say to the sixth angel who had the trumpet, "Release

the four angels bound at the great river Euphrates." [15] So the four angels who were prepared for the hour, day, month, and year were released to kill a third of the human race. [16] The number of mounted troops was two hundred million; I heard their number. [17] This is how I saw the horses and their riders in the vision: They had breastplates that were fiery red, hyacinth blue, and sulfur yellow. The heads of the horses were like the heads of lions, and from their mouths came fire, smoke, and sulfur. [18] A third of the human race was killed by these three plagues—by the fire, the smoke, and the sulfur that came from their mouths. [19] For the power of the horses is in their mouths and in their tails, because their tails, which resemble snakes, have heads that inflict injury.

[20] The rest of the people, who were not killed by these plagues, did not repent of the works of their hands to stop worshiping demons and idols of gold, silver, bronze, stone, and wood, which cannot see, hear, or walk. [21] And they did not repent of their murders, their sorceries, their sexual immorality, or their thefts.

❤ GOING DEEPER

1 Corinthians 15:51–52

[51] Listen, I am telling you a mystery: We will not all fall asleep, but we will all be changed, [52] in a moment, in the twinkling of an eye, at the last trumpet. For the trumpet will sound, and the dead will be raised incorruptible, and we will be changed.

1 Peter 3:8–12

DO NO EVIL

[8] Finally, all of you be like-minded and sympathetic, love one another, and be compassionate and humble, [9] not paying back evil for evil or insult for insult but, on the contrary, giving a blessing, since you were called for this, so that you may inherit a blessing.

[10] For the one who wants to love life
and to see good days,
let him keep his tongue from evil
and his lips from speaking deceit,
[11] and let him turn away from evil
and do what is good.
Let him seek peace and pursue it,
[12] because the eyes of the Lord are on the righteous
and his ears are open to their prayer.
But the face of the Lord is against
those who do what is evil.

The Seven Trumpets

Use the references provided to fill in what happens when each trumpet sounds in Revelation 8–11.

1	Rv 8:7	**2**	Rv 8:8–9	**3**	Rv 8:10–11

4	Rv 8:12–13	5	Rv 9:1–12	6	Rv 9:13–21	7	Rv 11:15–19

Take this day to catch up on your reading,
pray, and rest in the presence of the Lord.

WHEN THIS CORRUPTIBLE BODY IS CLOTHED WITH
INCORRUPTIBILITY, AND THIS MORTAL BODY IS CLOTHED WITH
IMMORTALITY, THEN THE SAYING THAT IS WRITTEN WILL TAKE PLACE:

DEATH HAS BEEN SWALLOWED UP IN VICTORY.
WHERE, DEATH, IS YOUR VICTORY?
WHERE, DEATH, IS YOUR STING?

THE STING OF DEATH IS SIN, AND THE POWER OF
SIN IS THE LAW. BUT THANKS BE TO GOD, WHO GIVES
US THE VICTORY THROUGH OUR LORD JESUS CHRIST!

1 Corinthians 15:54–57

Weekly Truth

Scripture is God breathed and true. When we memorize it, we carry the good news of Jesus with us wherever we go.

Throughout this plan, we will memorize verses that remind us of the holiness of God and call us to worship Him. This week, spend time memorizing Revelation 7:10.

**AND THEY CRIED OUT IN A LOUD VOICE:
SALVATION BELONGS TO OUR GOD,
WHO IS SEATED ON THE THRONE,
AND TO THE LAMB!**

Revelation 7:10

See tips for memorizing Scripture on page 120.

NOTES   Date

SHE READS TRUTH   DAY 7   51

The Seventh Trumpet

Use the worksheet found on page 46 to take notes as you read.

Revelation 10

THE MIGHTY ANGEL AND THE SMALL SCROLL

[1] Then I saw another mighty angel coming down from heaven, wrapped in a cloud, with a rainbow over his head. His face was like the sun, his legs were like pillars of fire, [2] and he held a little scroll opened in his hand. He put his right foot on the sea, his left on the land, [3] and he called out with a loud voice like a roaring lion. When he cried out, the seven thunders raised their voices. [4] And when the seven thunders spoke, I was about to write, but I heard a voice from heaven, saying, "Seal up what the seven thunders said, and do not write it down!"

[5] Then the angel that I had seen standing on the sea and on the land raised his right hand to heaven. [6] He swore by the one who lives forever and ever, who created heaven and what is in it, the earth and what is in it, and the sea and what is in it, "There will no longer be a delay, [7] but in the days when the seventh angel will blow his trumpet, then the mystery of God will be completed, as he announced to his servants the prophets."

[8] Then the voice that I heard from heaven spoke to me again and said, "Go, take the scroll that lies open in the hand of the angel who is standing on the sea and on the land."

[9] So I went to the angel and asked him to give me the little scroll. He said to me, "Take and eat it; it will be bitter in your stomach, but it will be as sweet as honey in your mouth."

[10] Then I took the little scroll from the angel's hand and ate it. It was as sweet as honey in my mouth, but when I ate it, my stomach became bitter. [11] And they said to me, "You must prophesy again about many peoples, nations, languages, and kings."

Revelation 11

THE TWO WITNESSES

[1] Then I was given a measuring reed like a rod, with these words: "Go and measure the temple of God and the altar, and count those who worship there. [2] But exclude the courtyard outside the temple. Don't measure it, because it is given to the nations, and they will trample the holy city for forty-two months. [3] I will grant my two witnesses authority to prophesy for 1,260 days, dressed in sackcloth." [4] These are the two olive trees and the two lampstands that stand before the Lord of the earth. [5] If anyone wants to harm them, fire comes from their mouths and consumes their enemies;

if anyone wants to harm them, he must be killed in this way. [6] They have authority to close up the sky so that it does not rain during the days of their prophecy. They also have power over the waters to turn them into blood and to strike the earth with every plague whenever they want.

THE WITNESSES MARTYRED

[7] When they finish their testimony, the beast that comes up out of the abyss will make war on them, conquer them, and kill them. [8] Their dead bodies will lie in the main street of the great city, which figuratively is called Sodom and Egypt, where also their Lord was crucified. [9] And some of the peoples, tribes, languages, and nations will view their bodies for three and a half days and not permit their bodies to be put into a tomb. [10] Those who live on the earth will gloat over them and celebrate and send gifts to one another because these two prophets had tormented those who live on the earth.

THE WITNESSES RESURRECTED

[11] But after three and a half days, the breath of life from God entered them, and they stood on their feet. Great fear fell on those who saw them. [12] Then they heard a loud voice from heaven saying to them, "Come up here." They went up to heaven in a cloud, while their enemies watched them. [13] At that moment a violent earthquake took place, a tenth of the city fell, and seven thousand people were killed in the earthquake. The survivors were terrified and gave glory to the God of heaven.

[14] The second woe has passed. Take note: The third woe is coming soon!

THE SEVENTH TRUMPET

[15] The seventh angel blew his trumpet, and there were loud voices in heaven saying,

THE KINGDOM OF THE WORLD HAS BECOME THE KINGDOM OF OUR LORD AND OF HIS CHRIST, AND HE WILL REIGN FOREVER AND EVER.

[16] The twenty-four elders, who were seated before God on their thrones, fell facedown and worshiped God, [17] saying,

We give you thanks, Lord God, the Almighty,
who is and who was,
because you have taken your great power
and have begun to reign.

¹⁸ The nations were angry,
but your wrath has come.
The time has come
for the dead to be judged
and to give the reward
to your servants the prophets,
to the saints, and to those who fear your name,
both small and great,
and the time has come to destroy
those who destroy the earth.

¹⁹ Then the temple of God in heaven was opened, and the ark of his covenant appeared in his temple. There were flashes of lightning, rumblings and peals of thunder, an earthquake, and severe hail.

♥ GOING DEEPER

Psalm 2
CORONATION OF THE SON

¹ Why do the nations rage
and the peoples plot in vain?
² The kings of the earth take their stand,
and the rulers conspire together
against the LORD and his Anointed One:
³ "Let's tear off their chains
and throw their ropes off of us."

⁴ The one enthroned in heaven laughs;
the Lord ridicules them.
⁵ Then he speaks to them in his anger
and terrifies them in his wrath:
⁶ "I have installed my king
on Zion, my holy mountain."

⁷ I will declare the LORD's decree.
He said to me, "You are my Son;
today I have become your Father.
⁸ Ask of me,
and I will make the nations your inheritance
and the ends of the earth your possession.
⁹ You will break them with an iron scepter;
you will shatter them like pottery."

¹⁰ So now, kings, be wise;
receive instruction, you judges of the earth.
¹¹ Serve the LORD with reverential awe
and rejoice with trembling.
¹² Pay homage to the Son or he will be angry
and you will perish in your rebellion,
for his anger may ignite at any moment.
All who take refuge in him are happy.

Daniel 2:36–44

³⁶ This was the dream; now we will tell the king its interpretation. ³⁷ Your Majesty, you are king of kings. The God of the heavens has given you sovereignty, power, strength, and glory. ³⁸ Wherever people live—or wild animals, or birds of the sky—he has handed them over to you and made you ruler over them all. You are the head of gold.

³⁹ After you, there will arise another kingdom, inferior to yours, and then another, a third kingdom, of bronze, which will rule the whole earth. ⁴⁰ A fourth kingdom will be as strong as iron; for iron crushes and shatters everything, and like iron that smashes, it will crush and smash all the others. ⁴¹ You saw the feet and toes, partly of a potter's fired clay and partly of iron—it will be a divided kingdom, though some of the strength of iron will be in it. You saw the iron mixed with clay, ⁴² and that the toes of the feet were partly iron and partly fired clay—part of the kingdom will be strong, and part will be brittle. ⁴³ You saw the iron mixed with clay—the peoples will mix with one another but will not hold together, just as iron does not mix with fired clay.

⁴⁴ In the days of those kings, the God of the heavens will set up a kingdom that will never be destroyed, and this kingdom will not be left to another people. It will crush all these kingdoms and bring them to an end, but will itself endure forever.

Revelation

AND THE

Old Testament

———

The book of Revelation contains few quotations from the Old Testament. However, scholars estimate nearly 70 percent of the 404 verses in Revelation contain Old Testament references, with as many as 750 allusions to and echoes of the Hebrew Scriptures—more than any other book in the New Testament. The following graphic is a visual approximation of the Old Testament allusions in the book of Revelation.

DAY 9

The Woman, the Child, and the Dragon

Revelation 12

THE WOMAN, THE CHILD, AND THE DRAGON

¹ A great sign appeared in heaven: a woman clothed with the sun, with the moon under her feet and a crown of twelve stars on her head. ² She was pregnant and cried out in labor and agony as she was about to give birth. ³ Then another sign appeared in heaven: There was a great fiery red dragon having seven heads and ten horns, and on its heads were seven crowns. ⁴ Its tail swept away a third of the stars in heaven and hurled them to the earth. And the dragon stood in front of the woman who was about to give birth, so that when she did give birth it might devour her child. ⁵ She gave birth to a Son, a male who is going to rule all nations with an iron rod. Her child was caught up to God and to his throne. ⁶ The woman fled into the wilderness, where she had a place prepared by God, to be nourished there for 1,260 days.

THE SALVATION AND THE POWER
AND THE KINGDOM OF OUR GOD
AND THE AUTHORITY OF HIS CHRIST
HAVE NOW COME...

Revelation 12:10

THE DRAGON THROWN OUT OF HEAVEN

[7] Then war broke out in heaven: Michael and his angels fought against the dragon. The dragon and his angels also fought, [8] but he could not prevail, and there was no place for them in heaven any longer. [9] So the great dragon was thrown out—the ancient serpent, who is called the devil and Satan, the one who deceives the whole world. He was thrown to earth, and his angels with him. [10] Then I heard a loud voice in heaven say,

> The salvation and the power
> and the kingdom of our God
> and the authority of his Christ
> have now come,
> because the accuser of our brothers and sisters,
> who accuses them
> before our God day and night,
> has been thrown down.
> [11] They conquered him
> by the blood of the Lamb
> and by the word of their testimony;
> for they did not love their lives
> to the point of death.
> [12] Therefore rejoice, you heavens,
> and you who dwell in them!
> Woe to the earth and the sea,
> because the devil has come down to you
> with great fury,
> because he knows his time is short.

THE WOMAN PERSECUTED

[13] When the dragon saw that he had been thrown down to the earth, he persecuted the woman who had given birth to the male child. [14] The woman was given two wings of a great eagle, so that she could fly from the serpent's presence to her place in the wilderness, where she was nourished for a time, times, and half a time. [15] From his

mouth the serpent spewed water like a river flowing after the woman, to sweep her away with a flood. ¹⁶ But the earth helped the woman. The earth opened its mouth and swallowed up the river that the dragon had spewed from his mouth. ¹⁷ So the dragon was furious with the woman and went off to wage war against the rest of her offspring—those who keep the commands of God and hold firmly to the testimony about Jesus.

THE BEAST FROM THE SEA

¹⁸ The dragon stood on the sand of the sea.

💜 GOING DEEPER

Genesis 3:1–15

THE TEMPTATION AND THE FALL

¹ Now the serpent was the most cunning of all the wild animals that the Lᴏʀᴅ God had made. He said to the woman, "Did God really say, 'You can't eat from any tree in the garden'?"

² The woman said to the serpent, "We may eat the fruit from the trees in the garden. ³ But about the fruit of the tree in the middle of the garden, God said, 'You must not eat it or touch it, or you will die.'"

⁴ "No! You will certainly not die," the serpent said to the woman. ⁵ "In fact, God knows that when you eat it your eyes will be opened and you will be like God, knowing good and evil." ⁶ The woman saw that the tree was good for food and delightful to look at, and that it was desirable for obtaining wisdom. So she took some of its fruit and ate it; she also gave some to her husband, who was with her, and he ate it. ⁷ Then the eyes of both of them were opened, and they knew they were naked; so they sewed fig leaves together and made coverings for themselves.

SIN'S CONSEQUENCES

⁸ Then the man and his wife heard the sound of the Lᴏʀᴅ God walking in the garden at the time of the evening breeze, and they hid from the Lᴏʀᴅ God among the trees of the garden. ⁹ So the Lᴏʀᴅ God called out to the man and said to him, "Where are you?"

¹⁰ And he said, "I heard you in the garden, and I was afraid because I was naked, so I hid."

¹¹ Then he asked, "Who told you that you were naked? Did you eat from the tree that I commanded you not to eat from?"

¹² The man replied, "The woman you gave to be with me—she gave me some fruit from the tree, and I ate."

¹³ So the Lᴏʀᴅ God asked the woman, "What is this you have done?"

And the woman said, "The serpent deceived me, and I ate."

¹⁴ So the Lᴏʀᴅ God said to the serpent:

> Because you have done this,
> you are cursed more than any livestock
> and more than any wild animal.
> You will move on your belly
> and eat dust all the days of your life.
> ¹⁵ I will put hostility between you and the woman,
> and between your offspring and her offspring.
> He will strike your head,
> and you will strike his heel.

Colossians 2:13–15

¹³ And when you were dead in trespasses and in the uncircumcision of your flesh, he made you alive with him and forgave us all our trespasses. ¹⁴ He erased the certificate of debt, with its obligations, that was against us and opposed to us, and has taken it away by nailing it to the cross. ¹⁵ He disarmed the rulers and authorities and disgraced them publicly; he triumphed over them in him.

NOTES	Date

DAY 10

The Beast from the Sea and the Beast from the Earth

Revelation 13

[1] And I saw a beast coming up out of the sea. It had ten horns and seven heads. On its horns were ten crowns, and on its heads were blasphemous names. [2] The beast I saw was like a leopard, its feet were like a bear's, and its mouth was like a lion's mouth. The dragon gave the beast his power, his throne, and great authority. [3] One of its heads appeared to be fatally wounded, but its fatal wound was healed.

The whole earth was amazed and followed the beast. [4] They worshiped the dragon because he gave authority to the beast. And they worshiped the beast, saying, "Who is like the beast? Who is able to wage war against it?"

5 The beast was given a mouth to utter boasts and blasphemies. It was allowed to exercise authority for forty-two months. 6 It began to speak blasphemies against God: to blaspheme his name and his dwelling—those who dwell in heaven. 7 And it was permitted to wage war against the saints and to conquer them. It was also given authority over every tribe, people, language, and nation. 8 All those who live on the earth will worship it, everyone whose name was not written from the foundation of the world in the book of life of the Lamb who was slaughtered.

9 If anyone has ears to hear, let him listen.

10 If anyone is to be taken captive,
into captivity he goes.
If anyone is to be killed with a sword,
with a sword he will be killed.

THIS CALLS FOR ENDURANCE AND FAITHFULNESS FROM THE SAINTS.

THE BEAST FROM THE EARTH

11 Then I saw another beast coming up out of the earth; it had two horns like a lamb, but it spoke like a dragon. 12 It exercises all the authority of the first beast on its behalf and compels the earth and those who live on it to worship the first beast, whose fatal wound was healed. 13 It also performs great signs, even causing fire to come down from heaven to earth in front of people. 14 It deceives those who live on the earth because of the signs that it is permitted to perform in the presence of the beast, telling those who live on the earth to make an image of the beast who was wounded by the sword and yet lived. 15 It was permitted to give breath to the image of the beast, so that the image of the beast could both speak and cause whoever would not worship the image of the beast to be killed. 16 And it makes everyone—small and great, rich and poor, free and slave—to receive a mark on his right hand or on his forehead, 17 so that no one can buy or sell unless he has the mark: the beast's name or the number of its name.

18 This calls for wisdom: Let the one who has understanding calculate the number of the beast, because it is the number of a person. Its number is 666.

Proverbs 1:7

The fear of the LORD
is the beginning of knowledge;
fools despise wisdom and discipline.

Hebrews 10:32–39

[32] Remember the earlier days when, after you had been enlightened, you endured a hard struggle with sufferings. [33] Sometimes you were publicly exposed to taunts and afflictions, and at other times you were companions of those who were treated that way. [34] For you sympathized with the prisoners and accepted with joy the confiscation of your possessions, because you know that you yourselves have a better and enduring possession. [35] So don't throw away your confidence, which has a great reward. [36] For you need endurance, so that after you have done God's will, you may receive what was promised.

[37] For yet in a very little while,
the Coming One will come and not delay.
[38] But my righteous one will live by faith;
and if he draws back,
I have no pleasure in him.

[39] But we are not those who draw back and are destroyed, but those who have faith and are saved.

Interpreting Revelation

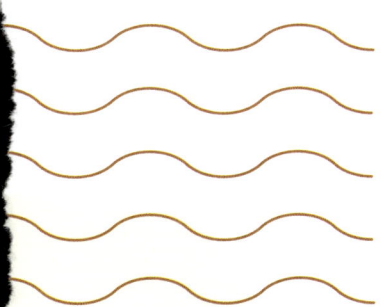

How do we approach a book that has a beast rising out of the sea, a slain Lamb opening a scroll, and a golden city descending to earth in the shape of a cube? How do we understand a woman seated on seven hills, a dragon whose tail sweeps a third of the stars from heaven, and a returning King with a sword in His mouth? Since it was written, Revelation has stirred up no shortage of opinions or speculation. This chart and the pages that follow show the most popular models for interpreting this final book of the New Testament.

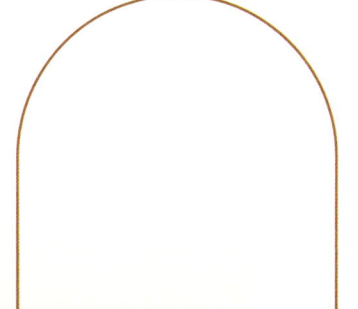

VISIONS IN REVELATION

CHAPTERS 1–3
Letters to the seven churches

CHAPTERS 4–11
Seals, trumpets, witnesses

INTERPRETATION

	CHAPTERS 1–3	CHAPTERS 4–11
P	First century churches	Jerusalem's destruction in AD 70
F	First century churches	Tribulation
H	First century churches	The church age, which either incorporates the millennial reign of Christ or culminates in the millennium
I	First century churches	The church age, over which Christ reigns (the millennium)

KEY

P — Partial-Preterist View

F — Futurist View

H — Historicist View

I — Idealist View

CHAPTERS 12–19

Woman, dragon, beasts, bowls, harlot, Armageddon

CHAPTER 20:1–6

Millennium

CHAPTERS 20:7–22:5

Dragon destroyed, all in graves rise, white throne judgment, all things new

P	Rome's fall in the fourth century

P	Remainder of the church age

P	The second coming, general resurrection, last judgment, new heaven and earth

F	Christ's 1,000-year reign on earth

F	The general resurrection, last judgment, new heaven and earth

H	The second coming, general resurrection, last judgment, new heaven and earth

I	The second coming, general resurrection, last judgment, new heaven and earth

PARTIAL-PRETERIST VIEW

According to this theory, most of the events depicted in Revelation occurred in the first century in connection with the destruction of Jerusalem and the temple in AD 70. Preterists argue for a date prior to AD 70 for the book's composition.

FUTURIST VIEW

In the view of futurists, Revelation 4–22 depict events in the distant future from John's perspective (though many futurists believe they may be in our near future). Dispensational premillennialists believe the resurrection of believers and the rapture of the Church will take place prior to the tribulation, while historical premillennialists believe the resurrection of believers and the rapture will take place at Christ's second coming, just prior to His millennial reign.

HISTORICIST VIEW

Historicists see Revelation 6:1–20:6 as detailing historical events throughout the church age: some past, some present, and some yet future.

IDEALIST VIEW

In this tradition, Revelation is seen as a symbolic depiction of the ongoing battle between good and evil throughout the church age. Idealists are hesitant to assign specific historical events to the symbolic visions John records.

ECLECTIC VIEW

This view holds the preterist, idealist, and futurist views in tension, noting the already-and-not-yet nature of God's kingdom.

The Millennial Reign

One of the most pivotal and controversial events in Revelation is the millennial reign of Christ, depicted in 20:1–6. Some see this thousand-year period as literal, while others see it as largely symbolic, referring either to the church age as a whole or the eternal age to come. Following are timelines of the major viewpoints.

CLASSICAL PREMILLENNIALISM

Classical premillennialism is a futurist view in which Christ will return before the millennium but after the great tribulation. Satan will be bound before the millennium but set loose afterward for a final war that will end with him being cast into the lake of fire.

CHURCH AGE

PRETRIBULATIONAL PREMILLENNIALISM

Also holding to a futurist viewpoint, pretribulational premillennialists believe that Christ will return before the millennium but also again before the tribulation, ensuring that believers will be spared the suffering that will take place during those years.

CHURCH AGE

POSTMILLENNIALISM

Compatible with both preterism and historicism, postmillennialism is the belief that the return of Christ will take place after the millennium. Classical postmillennialists see the thousand-year reign of Christ as the still-future, final stage of human history, distinct from the present age, in which the gospel has so permeated society that the world is fundamentally transformed. Other postmillennialists see the millennium as synonymous with the church age, when God's kingdom expands its geography and influence until the earth is "filled with the knowledge of the LORD's glory" (Hab 2:14).

CHURCH AGE

AMILLENNIALISM

Often argued by idealists but also compatible with historicism and preterism, amillennialism is the belief that when Revelation speaks of the thousand-year reign of Christ, it refers to Christ's reign over His people now (understanding "a thousand years" merely to denote a long period of time). In this view, Satan is currently being bound as the kingdom of God advances through the spread of the gospel.

CHURCH AGE/ MILLENNIUM

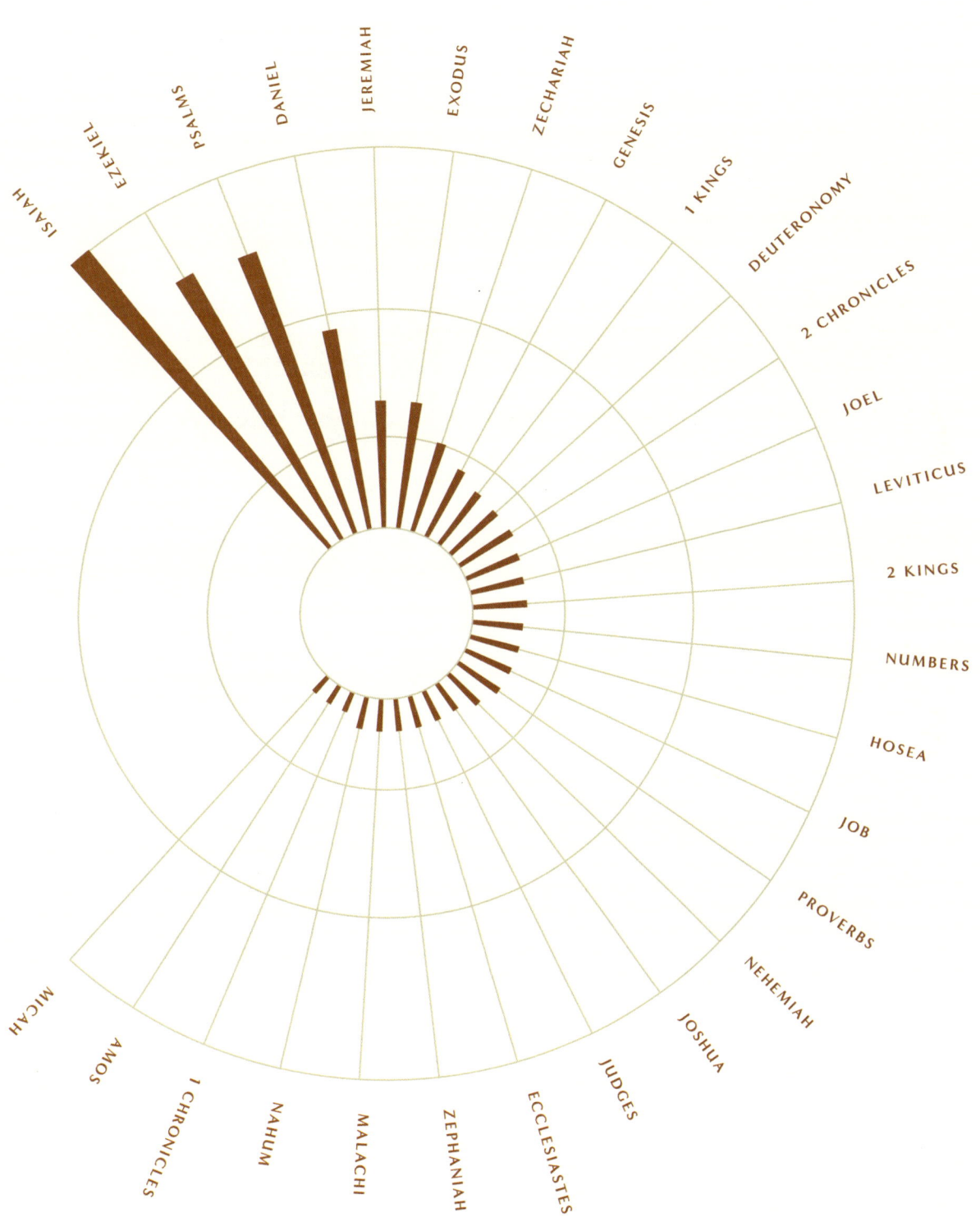

ISAIAH
EZEKIEL
PSALMS
DANIEL
JEREMIAH
EXODUS
ZECHARIAH
GENESIS
1 KINGS
DEUTERONOMY
2 CHRONICLES
JOEL
LEVITICUS
2 KINGS
NUMBERS
HOSEA
JOB
PROVERBS
NEHEMIAH
JOSHUA
JUDGES
ECCLESIASTES
ZEPHANIAH
MALACHI
NAHUM
1 CHRONICLES
AMOS
MICAH

TRIBULATION   MILLENNIUM   ETERNAL STATE

Resurrection of believers
Catching up of believers with Christ

Resurrection of nonbelievers
Judgment

TRIBULATION   MILLENNIUM   ETERNAL STATE

Resurrection of believers
Catching up of believers
with Christ

Believers return with Christ

Resurrection of nonbelievers
Judgment
New heaven, new earth

MILLENNIUM   ETERNAL STATE

Resurrection of believers
Catching up of believers with Christ
Resurrection of nonbelievers
Judgment
New heaven, new earth

ETERNAL STATE

Resurrection of believers
Catching up of believers with Christ
Resurrection of nonbelievers
Judgment
New heaven, new earth

DAY 11

The Proclamation of Three Angels

Revelation 14

THE LAMB AND THE 144,000

¹ Then I looked, and there was the Lamb, standing on Mount Zion, and with him were 144,000 who had his name and his Father's name written on their foreheads. ² I heard a sound from heaven like the sound of cascading waters and like the rumbling of loud thunder. The sound I heard was like harpists playing on their harps. ³ They sang a new song before the throne and before the four living creatures and the elders, but no one could learn the song except the 144,000 who had been redeemed from the earth. ⁴ These are the ones who have not defiled themselves with women, since they remained virgins. These are the ones who follow the Lamb wherever he goes. They were redeemed from humanity as the firstfruits for God and the Lamb. ⁵ No lie was found in their mouths; they are blameless.

THE PROCLAMATION OF THREE ANGELS

⁶ Then I saw another angel flying high overhead, with the eternal gospel to announce to the inhabitants of the earth—to every nation, tribe, language, and people. ⁷ He spoke with a loud voice: "Fear God and give him glory, because the hour of his judgment has come. Worship the one who made heaven and earth, the sea and the springs of water."

⁸ And another, a second angel, followed, saying, "It has fallen, Babylon the Great has fallen. She made all the nations drink the wine of her sexual immorality, which brings wrath."

⁹ And another, a third angel, followed them and spoke with a loud voice: "If anyone worships the beast and its image and receives a mark on his forehead or on his hand, ¹⁰ he will also drink the wine of God's wrath, which is poured full strength into the cup of his anger. He will be tormented with fire and sulfur in the sight of the holy angels and in the sight of the Lamb, ¹¹ and the smoke of their torment will go up forever and ever. There is no rest day or night for those who worship the beast and its image, or anyone who receives the mark of its name. ¹² This calls for endurance from the saints, who keep God's commands and their faith in Jesus."

¹³ Then I heard a voice from heaven saying, "Write: Blessed are the dead who die in the Lord from now on."

"Yes," says the Spirit, "so they will rest from their labors, since their works follow them."

REAPING THE EARTH'S HARVEST

¹⁴ Then I looked, and there was a white cloud, and one like the Son of Man was seated on the cloud, with a golden crown on his head and a sharp sickle in his hand. ¹⁵ Another angel came out of the temple, crying out in a loud voice to the one who was seated on the cloud, "Use your sickle and reap, for the time to reap has come, since the harvest of the earth is ripe." ¹⁶ So the one seated on the cloud swung his sickle over the earth, and the earth was harvested.

¹⁷ Then another angel who also had a sharp sickle came out of the temple in heaven. ¹⁸ Yet another angel, who had authority over fire, came from the altar, and he called with a loud voice to the one who had the sharp sickle, "Use your sharp sickle and gather the clusters of grapes from the vineyard of the earth, because its grapes have ripened." ¹⁹ So the angel swung his sickle at the earth and gathered the grapes from the vineyard of the earth, and he threw them into the great winepress of God's wrath. ²⁰ Then the press was trampled outside the city, and blood flowed out of the press up to the horses' bridles for about 180 miles.

Psalm 107:1–3

THANKSGIVING FOR GOD'S DELIVERANCE

¹ GIVE THANKS TO THE LORD,
  FOR HE IS GOOD;
HIS FAITHFUL LOVE ENDURES FOREVER.
² LET THE REDEEMED OF THE
  LORD PROCLAIM
THAT HE HAS REDEEMED THEM
  FROM THE POWER OF THE FOE

³ and has gathered them from the lands—
from the east and the west,
from the north and the south.

Hebrews 12:18–24

¹⁸ For you have not come to what could be touched, to a blazing fire, to darkness, gloom, and storm, ¹⁹ to the blast of a trumpet, and the sound of words. Those who heard it begged that not another word be spoken to them, ²⁰ for they could not bear what was commanded: If even an animal touches the mountain, it must be stoned. ²¹ The appearance was so terrifying that Moses said, I am trembling with fear. ²² Instead, you have come to Mount Zion, to the city of the living God (the heavenly Jerusalem), to myriads of angels, a festive gathering, ²³ to the assembly of the firstborn whose names have been written in heaven, to a Judge, who is God of all, to the spirits of righteous people made perfect, ²⁴ and to Jesus, the mediator of a new covenant, and to the sprinkled blood, which says better things than the blood of Abel.

NOTES	Date

The Seven Bowls

Use the worksheet found on page 78 to take notes as you read.

Revelation 15

PREPARATION FOR THE BOWL JUDGMENTS

[1] Then I saw another great and awe-inspiring sign in heaven: seven angels with the seven last plagues; for with them God's wrath will be completed. [2] I also saw something like a sea of glass mixed with fire, and those who had won the victory over the beast, its image, and the number of its name, were standing on the sea of glass with harps from God. [3] They sang the song of God's servant Moses and the song of the Lamb:

> Great and awe-inspiring are your works,
> Lord God, the Almighty;
> just and true are your ways,
> King of the nations.
> [4] Lord, who will not fear
> and glorify your name?
> For you alone are holy.
> All the nations will come
> and worship before you
> because your righteous acts
> have been revealed.

[5] After this I looked, and the heavenly temple—the tabernacle of testimony—was opened. [6] Out of the temple came the seven angels with the seven plagues, dressed in pure, bright linen, with golden sashes wrapped around their chests.

[7] One of the four living creatures gave the seven angels seven golden bowls filled with the wrath of God who lives forever and ever. [8] Then the temple was filled with smoke from the glory of God and from his power, and no one could enter the temple until the seven plagues of the seven angels were completed.

Revelation 16

THE FIRST BOWL

[1] Then I heard a loud voice from the temple saying to the seven angels, "Go and pour out the seven bowls of God's wrath on the earth." [2] The first went and poured out his bowl on the earth, and severely painful sores broke out on the people who had the mark of the beast and who worshiped its image.

THE SECOND BOWL

[3] The second poured out his bowl into the sea. It turned to blood like that of a dead person, and all life in the sea died.

THE THIRD BOWL

[4] The third poured out his bowl into the rivers and the springs of water, and they became blood. [5] I heard the angel of the waters say,

You are just,

the Holy One, who is and who was,

because you have passed judgment on these things.

⁶ Because they poured out

the blood of the saints and the prophets,

you have given them blood to drink;

they deserve it!

⁷ I heard the altar say,

YES, LORD GOD, THE ALMIGHTY, TRUE AND JUST ARE YOUR JUDGMENTS.

THE FOURTH BOWL

⁸ The fourth poured out his bowl on the sun. It was allowed to scorch people with fire, ⁹ and people were scorched by the intense heat. So they blasphemed the name of God, who has the power over these plagues, and they did not repent and give him glory.

THE FIFTH BOWL

¹⁰ The fifth poured out his bowl on the throne of the beast, and its kingdom was plunged into darkness. People gnawed their tongues because of their pain ¹¹ and blasphemed the God of heaven because of their pains and their sores, but they did not repent of their works.

THE SIXTH BOWL

¹² The sixth poured out his bowl on the great river Euphrates, and its water was dried up to prepare the way for the kings from the east. ¹³ Then I saw three unclean spirits like frogs coming from the dragon's mouth, from the beast's mouth, and from the mouth of the false prophet. ¹⁴ For they are demonic spirits performing signs, who travel to the kings of the whole world to assemble them for the battle on the great day of God, the Almighty. ¹⁵ "Look, I am coming like a thief. Blessed is the one who is alert and remains clothed so that he may not go around naked and people see his shame." ¹⁶ So they assembled the kings at the place called in Hebrew, Armageddon.

THE SEVENTH BOWL

¹⁷ Then the seventh poured out his bowl into the air, and a loud voice came out of the temple from the throne, saying, "It is done!" ¹⁸ There were flashes of lightning, rumblings, and peals of thunder. And a severe earthquake occurred like no other since people have been on the earth, so great was the quake. ¹⁹ The great city split into three parts, and the cities of the nations fell. Babylon the Great was remembered in God's presence; he gave her the cup filled with the wine of his fierce anger. ²⁰ Every island fled, and the mountains disappeared. ²¹ Enormous hailstones,

each weighing about a hundred pounds, fell from the sky on people, and they blasphemed God for the plague of hail because that plague was extremely severe.

◆ GOING DEEPER

Exodus 15:1–18

ISRAEL'S SONG

¹ Then Moses and the Israelites sang this song to the Lord. They said:

> I will sing to the Lord,
> for he is highly exalted;
> he has thrown the horse
> and its rider into the sea.
> ² The Lord is my strength and my song;
> he has become my salvation.
> This is my God, and I will praise him,
> my father's God, and I will exalt him.
> ³ The Lord is a warrior;
> the Lord is his name.

> ⁴ He threw Pharaoh's chariots
> and his army into the sea;
> the elite of his officers
> were drowned in the Red Sea.
> ⁵ The floods covered them;
> they sank to the depths like a stone.
> ⁶ Lord, your right hand is glorious in power.
> Lord, your right hand shattered the enemy.
> ⁷ You overthrew your adversaries
> by your great majesty.
> You unleashed your burning wrath;
> it consumed them like stubble.
> ⁸ The water heaped up at the blast from your nostrils;
> the currents stood firm like a dam.
> The watery depths congealed in the heart of the sea.

> ⁹ The enemy said:
> "I will pursue, I will overtake,
> I will divide the spoil.
> My desire will be gratified at their expense.
> I will draw my sword;
> my hand will destroy them."
> ¹⁰ But you blew with your breath,
> and the sea covered them.
> They sank like lead
> in the mighty waters.

> ¹¹ Lord, who is like you among the gods?
> Who is like you, glorious in holiness,
> revered with praises, performing wonders?
> ¹² You stretched out your right hand,
> and the earth swallowed them.
> ¹³ With your faithful love,
> you will lead the people
> you have redeemed;
> you will guide them to your holy dwelling
> with your strength.

> ¹⁴ When the peoples hear, they will shudder;
> anguish will seize the inhabitants of Philistia.
> ¹⁵ Then the chiefs of Edom will be terrified;
> trembling will seize the leaders of Moab;
> all the inhabitants of Canaan will panic;
> ¹⁶ terror and dread will fall on them.
> They will be as still as a stone
> because of your powerful arm
> until your people pass by, Lord,
> until the people whom you purchased pass by.

> ¹⁷ You will bring them in and plant them
> on the mountain of your possession;
> Lord, you have prepared the place
> for your dwelling;
> Lord, your hands have established the sanctuary.
> ¹⁸ The Lord will reign forever and ever!

The Seven Bowls

Use the references provided to fill in the descriptions of the seven bowls in Revelation 16.

1	Rv 16:1–2	2	Rv 16:3	3	Rv 16:4–7

4	Rv 16:8–9	5	Rv 16:10–11	6	Rv 16:12–16	7	Rv 16:17–21

Take this day to catch up on your reading,
pray, and rest in the presence of the Lord.

GIVE THANKS TO THE LORD, FOR HE IS GOOD;
HIS FAITHFUL LOVE ENDURES FOREVER.
LET THE REDEEMED OF THE LORD PROCLAIM
THAT HE HAS REDEEMED THEM FROM THE POWER OF THE FOE
AND HAS GATHERED THEM FROM THE LANDS—
FROM THE EAST AND THE WEST,
FROM THE NORTH AND THE SOUTH.

Psalm 107:1–3

Weekly Truth

Scripture is God breathed and true. When we memorize it, we carry the good news of Jesus with us wherever we go.

Throughout this plan, we are memorizing verses that remind us of the holiness of God and call us to worship Him. This week, spend time memorizing Revelation 16:7.

YES, LORD GOD, THE ALMIGHTY, TRUE AND JUST ARE YOUR JUDGMENTS.

Revelation 16:7

See tips for memorizing Scripture on page 120.

NOTES | Date

DAY 15

The Woman and the Scarlet Beast

Revelation 17

THE WOMAN AND THE SCARLET BEAST

¹ Then one of the seven angels who had the seven bowls came and spoke with me: "Come, I will show you the judgment of the notorious prostitute who is seated on many waters. ² The kings of the earth committed sexual immorality with her, and those who live on the earth became drunk on the wine of her sexual immorality." ³ Then he carried me away in the Spirit to a wilderness.

I saw a woman sitting on a scarlet beast that was covered with blasphemous names and had seven heads and ten horns. ⁴ The woman was dressed in purple and scarlet, adorned with gold, jewels, and pearls. She had a golden cup in her hand filled with everything detestable and with the impurities of her prostitution. ⁵ On her forehead was written a name,

THESE WILL MAKE WAR AGAINST THE LAMB, BUT
THE LAMB WILL CONQUER THEM BECAUSE HE IS
LORD OF LORDS AND KING OF KINGS. THOSE WITH
HIM ARE CALLED, CHOSEN, AND FAITHFUL.

Revelation 17:14

a mystery: BABYLON THE GREAT, THE MOTHER OF PROSTITUTES AND OF THE DETESTABLE THINGS OF THE EARTH. [6] Then I saw that the woman was drunk with the blood of the saints and with the blood of the witnesses to Jesus. When I saw her, I was greatly astonished.

THE MEANING OF THE WOMAN AND OF THE BEAST

[7] Then the angel said to me, "Why are you astonished? I will explain to you the mystery of the woman and of the beast, with the seven heads and the ten horns, that carries her. [8] The beast that you saw was, and is not, and is about to come up from the abyss and go to destruction. Those who live on the earth whose names have not been written in the book of life from the foundation of the world will be astonished when they see the beast that was, and is not, and is to come. [9] This calls for a mind that has wisdom.

"The seven heads are seven mountains on which the woman is seated. They are also seven kings: [10] Five have fallen, one is, the other has not yet come, and when he comes, he must remain for only a little while. [11] The beast that was and is not, is itself an eighth king, but it belongs to the seven and is going to destruction. [12] The ten horns you saw are ten kings who have not yet received a kingdom, but they will receive authority as kings with the beast for one hour. [13] These have one purpose, and they give their power and authority to the beast. [14] These will make war against the Lamb, but the Lamb will conquer them because he is Lord of lords and King of kings. Those with him are called, chosen, and faithful."

[15] He also said to me, "The waters you saw, where the prostitute was seated, are peoples, multitudes, nations, and languages. [16] The ten horns you saw, and the beast, will hate the prostitute. They will make her desolate and naked, devour her flesh, and burn her up with fire. [17] For God has put it into their hearts to carry out his plan by having one purpose and to give their kingdom to the beast until the words of God are fulfilled. [18] And the woman you saw is the great city that has royal power over the kings of the earth."

Psalm 90
ETERNAL GOD AND MORTAL MAN

A prayer of Moses, the man of God.

¹ Lord, you have been our refuge
in every generation.
² Before the mountains were born,
before you gave birth to the earth and the world,
from eternity to eternity, you are God.

³ You return mankind to the dust,
saying, "Return, descendants of Adam."
⁴ For in your sight a thousand years
are like yesterday that passes by,
like a few hours of the night.
⁵ You end their lives; they sleep.
They are like grass that grows in the morning—
⁶ in the morning it sprouts and grows;
by evening it withers and dries up.

⁷ For we are consumed by your anger;
we are terrified by your wrath.
⁸ You have set our iniquities before you,
our secret sins in the light of your presence.
⁹ For all our days ebb away under your wrath;
we end our years like a sigh.
¹⁰ Our lives last seventy years
or, if we are strong, eighty years.
Even the best of them are struggle and sorrow;
indeed, they pass quickly and we fly away.
¹¹ Who understands the power of your anger?
Your wrath matches the fear that is due you.
¹² Teach us to number our days carefully
so that we may develop wisdom in our hearts.

¹³ LORD—how long?
Turn and have compassion on your servants.
¹⁴ Satisfy us in the morning with your faithful love
so that we may shout with joy and be glad all our days.
¹⁵ Make us rejoice for as many days as you have humbled us,
for as many years as we have seen adversity.
¹⁶ Let your work be seen by your servants,
and your splendor by their children.
¹⁷ Let the favor of the Lord our God be on us;
establish for us the work of our hands—
establish the work of our hands!

1 Timothy 6:11–16
FIGHT THE GOOD FIGHT

¹¹ But you, man of God, flee from these things, and pursue righteousness, godliness, faith, love, endurance, and gentleness. ¹² Fight the good fight of the faith. Take hold of eternal life to which you were called and about which you have made a good confession in the presence of many witnesses. ¹³ In the presence of God, who gives life to all, and of Christ Jesus, who gave a good confession before Pontius Pilate, I charge you ¹⁴ to keep this command without fault or failure until the appearing of our Lord Jesus Christ. ¹⁵ God will bring this about in his own time. He is the blessed and only Sovereign, the King of kings, and the Lord of lords, ¹⁶ who alone is immortal and who lives in unapproachable light, whom no one has seen or can see, to him be honor and eternal power. Amen.

The Fall of Babylon

Revelation 18

THE FALL OF BABYLON THE GREAT

¹ After this I saw another angel with great authority coming down from heaven, and the earth was illuminated by his splendor. ² He called out in a mighty voice:

It has fallen,
Babylon the Great has fallen!
She has become a home for demons,
a haunt for every unclean spirit,
a haunt for every unclean bird,
and a haunt for every unclean and despicable beast.
³ For all the nations have drunk
the wine of her sexual immorality,
which brings wrath.
The kings of the earth
have committed sexual immorality with her,
and the merchants of the earth
have grown wealthy from her sensuality and excess.

⁴ Then I heard another voice from heaven:

Come out of her, my people,
so that you will not share in her sins
or receive any of her plagues.

⁵ For her sins are piled up to heaven,
and God has remembered her crimes.
⁶ Pay her back the way she also paid,
and double it according to her works.
In the cup in which she mixed,
mix a double portion for her.
⁷ As much as she glorified herself and indulged her sensual
and excessive ways,
give her that much torment and grief.
For she says in her heart,
"I sit as a queen;
I am not a widow,
and I will never see grief."
⁸ For this reason her plagues will come in just one day—
death and grief and famine.
She will be burned up with fire,
because the Lord God who judges her is mighty.

THE WORLD MOURNS BABYLON'S FALL

⁹ The kings of the earth who have committed sexual immorality and shared her sensual and excessive ways will weep and mourn over her when they see the smoke from her burning. ¹⁰ They will stand far off in fear of her torment, saying,

REJOICE OVER HER, HEAVEN, AND
YOU SAINTS, APOSTLES, AND PROPHETS,
BECAUSE GOD HAS PRONOUNCED ON HER
THE JUDGMENT SHE PASSED ON YOU!

Revelation 18:20

Woe, woe, the great city,
Babylon, the mighty city!
For in a single hour
your judgment has come.

[11] The merchants of the earth will weep and mourn over her, because no one buys their cargo any longer— [12] cargo of gold, silver, jewels, and pearls; fine linen, purple, silk, and scarlet; all kinds of fragrant wood products; objects of ivory; objects of expensive wood, brass, iron, and marble; [13] cinnamon, spice, incense, myrrh, and frankincense; wine, olive oil, fine flour, and grain; cattle and sheep; horses and carriages; and slaves—human lives.

[14] The fruit you craved has left you.
All your splendid and glamorous things are gone;
they will never find them again.

[15] The merchants of these things, who became rich from her, will stand far off in fear of her torment, weeping and mourning, [16] saying,

Woe, woe, the great city,
dressed in fine linen, purple, and scarlet,
adorned with gold, jewels, and pearls;
[17] for in a single hour
such fabulous wealth was destroyed!

And every shipmaster, seafarer, the sailors, and all who do business by sea, stood far off [18] as they watched the smoke from her burning and kept crying out, "Who was like the great city?" [19] They threw dust on their heads and kept crying out, weeping, and mourning,

Woe, woe, the great city,

where all those who have ships on the sea

became rich from her wealth;

for in a single hour she was destroyed.

²⁰ Rejoice over her, heaven,

and you saints, apostles, and prophets,

because God has pronounced on her the judgment she

passed on you!

THE FINALITY OF BABYLON'S FALL

²¹ Then a mighty angel picked up a stone like a large millstone and threw it into the sea, saying,

In this way, Babylon the great city

will be thrown down violently

and never be found again.

²² The sound of harpists, musicians,

flutists, and trumpeters

will never be heard in you again;

no craftsman of any trade

will ever be found in you again;

the sound of a mill

will never be heard in you again;

²³ the light of a lamp

will never shine in you again;

and the voice of a groom and bride

will never be heard in you again.

All this will happen

because your merchants

were the nobility of the earth,

because all the nations were deceived

by your sorcery.

²⁴ In her was found the blood of prophets and saints,

and of all those slaughtered on the earth.

🔖 GOING DEEPER

Isaiah 52:11

Leave, leave, go out from there!

Do not touch anything unclean;

go out from her, purify yourselves,

you who carry the vessels of the Lord.

Jeremiah 51:47–50

⁴⁷ Therefore, look, the days are coming

when I will punish Babylon's carved images.

Her entire land will suffer shame,

and all her slain will lie fallen within her.

⁴⁸ HEAVEN AND EARTH AND
EVERYTHING IN THEM
WILL SHOUT FOR JOY
OVER BABYLON
BECAUSE THE DESTROYERS
FROM THE NORTH
WILL COME AGAINST HER.

This is the Lord's declaration.

⁴⁹ Babylon must fall because of the slain of Israel,

even as the slain of the whole earth fell

because of Babylon.

⁵⁰ You who have escaped the sword,

go and do not stand still!

Remember the Lord from far away,

and let Jerusalem come to your mind.

NOTES	Date

Babylon the Great

AND THE

New Jerusalem

———

Revelation 17 and 18 describe the judgment of Babylon the Great, a city of wickedness. Known for idolatry and cruelty, the historical Babylon opposed and oppressed God's people throughout the Old Testament. In Revelation, Babylon likely symbolizes both the Roman Empire of the first century and the sinfulness of humanity across the globe and throughout history.

On the heels of this city's destruction, another city is depicted as descending from heaven—God's city, the new Jerusalem. On the following page is a summary of how the bride of Christ (God's redeemed people) and the new Jerusalem are contrasted with Babylon the Great in the book of Revelation.

THE WOMAN ON THE SCARLET BEAST AND BABYLON THE GREAT

Revelation 17–18

...the notorious prostitute. RV 17:1

...dressed in purple and scarlet. RV 17:4

...the great city that has royal power over the kings of the earth. RV 17:18

...a home for demons, a haunt for every unclean spirit, a haunt for every unclean bird, and a haunt for every unclean and despicable beast. RV 18:2

Come out of her, my people... RV 18:4

...her sins are piled up to heaven. RV 18:5

For this reason her plagues will come in just one day—death and grief and famine. She will be burned up with fire. RV 18:8

The kings of the earth...have committed sexual immorality and shared her sensual and excessive ways. RV 18:9

...all the nations were deceived by your sorcery. RV 18:23

THE BRIDE OF CHRIST AND THE NEW JERUSALEM

Revelation 19–22

...the bride, the wife of the Lamb. RV 21:9

She was given fine linen to wear, bright and pure. RV 19:8

...the holy city,...coming down out of heaven from God. RV 21:2

Nothing unclean will ever enter it. RV 21:27

Blessed are those who wash their robes, so that they may...enter the city by the gates. RV 22:14

...the righteous acts of the saints. RV 19:8

He will wipe away every tear from their eyes. Death will be no more; grief, crying, and pain will be no more, because the previous things have passed away. RV 21:4

...the kings of the earth will bring their glory into it. RV 21:24

The leaves of the tree [of life] are for healing the nations... RV 22:2

Celebration in Heaven

Revelation 19

CELEBRATION IN HEAVEN

¹ After this I heard something like the loud voice of a vast multitude in heaven, saying,

Hallelujah!
Salvation, glory, and power belong to our God,
² because his judgments are true and righteous,
because he has judged the notorious prostitute
who corrupted the earth with her
    sexual immorality;
and he has avenged the blood of his servants
that was on her hands.

³ A second time they said,

Hallelujah!
Her smoke ascends forever and ever!

⁴ Then the twenty-four elders and the four living creatures fell down and worshiped God, who is seated on the throne, saying,

Amen! Hallelujah!

⁵ A voice came from the throne, saying,

Praise our God,
all his servants, and the ones who fear him,
both small and great!

⁶ Then I heard something like the voice of a vast multitude, like the sound of cascading waters, and like the rumbling of loud thunder, saying,

Hallelujah, because our Lord God, the Almighty, reigns!
⁷ Let us be glad, rejoice, and give him glory,
because the marriage of the Lamb has come,
and his bride has prepared herself.
⁸ She was given fine linen to wear, bright and pure.

For the fine linen represents the righteous acts of the saints.

⁹ Then he said to me, "Write: Blessed are those invited to the marriage feast of the Lamb!" He also said to me, "These words of God are true." ¹⁰ Then I fell at his feet to worship him, but he said to me, "Don't do that! I am a fellow servant with you and your brothers and sisters who hold firmly to the testimony of Jesus. Worship God, because the testimony of Jesus is the spirit of prophecy."

[11] Then I saw heaven opened, and there was a white horse. Its rider is called Faithful and True, and with justice he judges and makes war. [12] His eyes were like a fiery flame, and many crowns were on his head. He had a name written that no one knows except himself. [13] He wore a robe dipped in blood, and his name is called the Word of God. [14] The armies that were in heaven followed him on white horses, wearing pure white linen. [15] A sharp sword came from his mouth, so that he might strike the nations with it. He will rule them with an iron rod. He will also trample the winepress of the fierce anger of God, the Almighty. [16] And he has a name written on his robe and on his thigh: KING OF KINGS AND LORD OF LORDS.

THE BEAST AND ITS ARMIES DEFEATED

[17] Then I saw an angel standing in the sun, and he called out in a loud voice, saying to all the birds flying high overhead, "Come, gather together for the great supper of God, [18] so that you may eat the flesh of kings, the flesh of military commanders, the flesh of the mighty, the flesh of horses and of their riders, and the flesh of everyone, both free and slave, small and great."

[19] Then I saw the beast, the kings of the earth, and their armies gathered together to wage war against the rider on the horse and against his army. [20] But the beast was taken prisoner, and along with it the false prophet, who had performed the signs in its presence. He deceived those who accepted the mark of the beast and those who worshiped its image with these signs. Both of them were thrown alive into the lake of fire that burns with sulfur. [21] The rest were killed with the sword that came from the mouth of the rider on the horse, and all the birds ate their fill of their flesh.

Revelation 20

SATAN BOUND

[1] Then I saw an angel coming down from heaven holding the key to the abyss and a great chain in his hand. [2] He seized the dragon, that ancient serpent who is the devil and Satan, and bound him for a thousand years. [3] He threw him into the abyss, closed it, and put a seal on it so that he would no longer deceive the nations until the thousand years were completed. After that, he must be released for a short time.

THE SAINTS REIGN WITH CHRIST

[4] Then I saw thrones, and people seated on them who were given authority to judge. I also saw the souls of those who had been beheaded because of their testimony about Jesus and because of the word of God, who had not worshiped the beast or his image, and who had not accepted the mark on their foreheads or their hands. They came to life and reigned with Christ for a thousand years. [5] The rest of the dead did not come to life until the thousand years were completed.

This is the first resurrection. [6] Blessed and holy is the one who shares in the first resurrection! The second death has no power over them, but they will be priests of God and of Christ, and they will reign with him for a thousand years.

SATANIC REBELLION CRUSHED

[7] When the thousand years are completed, Satan will be released from his prison [8] and will go out to deceive the nations at the four corners of the earth, Gog and Magog, to gather them for battle. Their number is like the sand of the sea. [9] They came up across the breadth of the earth and surrounded the encampment of the saints, the beloved city. Then fire came down from heaven and consumed them. [10] The devil who deceived them was thrown into the lake of fire and sulfur where the beast and the false prophet are, and they will be tormented day and night forever and ever.

THE GREAT WHITE THRONE JUDGMENT

[11] Then I saw a great white throne and one seated on it. Earth and heaven fled from his presence, and no place was found for them. [12] I also saw the dead, the great and the small, standing before the throne, and books were opened. Another book was opened, which is the book of life, and the dead were judged according to their works by what was written in the books. [13] Then the sea gave up the dead that were in it, and death and Hades gave up the dead that were in them; each one was judged according to their works. [14] Death and Hades were thrown into the lake of fire. This is the second death, the lake of fire. [15] And anyone whose name was not found written in the book of life was thrown into the lake of fire.

🔖 GOING DEEPER

Isaiah 25:6–9

[6] On this mountain,
the LORD of Armies will prepare for all the peoples a feast
   of choice meat,

a feast with aged wine, prime cuts of choice meat, fine
   vintage wine.
[7] On this mountain
he will swallow up the burial shroud,
the shroud over all the peoples,
the sheet covering all the nations.
[8] When he has swallowed up death once and for all,
the Lord GOD will wipe away the tears
from every face
and remove his people's disgrace
from the whole earth,
for the LORD has spoken.

[9] On that day it will be said,
"Look, this is our God;
we have waited for him, and he has saved us.
This is the LORD; we have waited for him.
Let's rejoice and be glad in his salvation."

Isaiah 54:5–7

[5] "Indeed, your husband is your Maker—
his name is the LORD of Armies—
and the Holy One of Israel is your Redeemer;
he is called the God of the whole earth.
[6] For the LORD has called you,
like a wife deserted and wounded in spirit,
a wife of one's youth when she is rejected,"
says your God.
[7] "I deserted you for a brief moment,
but I will take you back with abundant compassion."

Ephesians 5:25–27

[25] Husbands, love your wives, just as Christ loved the church and gave himself for her [26] to make her holy, cleansing her with the washing of water by the word. [27] He did this to present the church to himself in splendor, without spot or wrinkle or anything like that, but holy and blameless.

DAY 18

The New Creation

Use the worksheet found on
page 103 to take notes as you read.

Revelation 21

THE NEW CREATION

¹ Then I saw a new heaven and a new earth; for the first heaven and the first earth had passed away, and the sea was no more. ² I also saw the holy city, the new Jerusalem, coming down out of heaven from God, prepared like a bride adorned for her husband.

³ Then I heard a loud voice from the throne: Look, God's dwelling is with humanity, and he will live with them. They will be his peoples, and God himself will be with them and will be their God. ⁴ He will wipe away every tear from their eyes. Death will be no more; grief, crying, and pain will be no more, because the previous things have passed away.

THEN THE ONE SEATED ON THE THRONE SAID,
"LOOK, I AM MAKING EVERYTHING NEW."

Revelation 21:5

⁵ Then the one seated on the throne said, "Look, I am making everything new." He also said, "Write, because these words are faithful and true." ⁶ Then he said to me, "It is done! I am the Alpha and the Omega, the beginning and the end. I will freely give to the thirsty from the spring of the water of life. ⁷ The one who conquers will inherit these things, and I will be his God, and he will be my son. ⁸ But the cowards, faithless, detestable, murderers, sexually immoral, sorcerers, idolaters, and all liars—their share will be in the lake that burns with fire and sulfur, which is the second death."

THE NEW JERUSALEM

⁹ Then one of the seven angels, who had held the seven bowls filled with the seven last plagues, came and spoke with me: "Come, I will show you the bride, the wife of the Lamb." ¹⁰ He then carried me away in the Spirit to a great, high mountain and showed me the holy city, Jerusalem, coming down out of heaven from God, ¹¹ arrayed with God's glory. Her radiance was like a precious jewel, like a jasper stone, clear as crystal. ¹² The city had a massive high wall, with twelve gates. Twelve angels were at the gates; the names of the twelve tribes of Israel's sons were inscribed on the gates. ¹³ There were three gates on the east, three gates on the north, three gates on the south, and three gates on the west. ¹⁴ The city wall had twelve foundations, and the twelve names of the twelve apostles of the Lamb were on the foundations.

¹⁵ The one who spoke with me had a golden measuring rod to measure the city, its gates, and its wall. ¹⁶ The city is laid out in a square; its length and width are the same. He measured the city with the rod at 12,000 *stadia*. Its length, width, and height are equal. ¹⁷ Then he measured its wall, 144 cubits according to human measurement, which the angel used. ¹⁸ The building material of its wall was jasper, and the city was pure gold clear as glass. ¹⁹ The foundations of the city wall were adorned with every kind of jewel: the first foundation is jasper, the second sapphire,

the third chalcedony, the fourth emerald, [20] the fifth sardonyx, the sixth carnelian, the seventh chrysolite, the eighth beryl, the ninth topaz, the tenth chrysoprase, the eleventh jacinth, the twelfth amethyst. [21] The twelve gates are twelve pearls; each individual gate was made of a single pearl. The main street of the city was pure gold, transparent as glass.

[22] I DID NOT SEE A TEMPLE IN IT, BECAUSE THE LORD GOD THE ALMIGHTY AND THE LAMB ARE ITS TEMPLE.

[23] The city does not need the sun or the moon to shine on it, because the glory of God illuminates it, and its lamp is the Lamb. [24] The nations will walk by its light, and the kings of the earth will bring their glory into it. [25] Its gates will never close by day because it will never be night there. [26] They will bring the glory and honor of the nations into it. [27] Nothing unclean will ever enter it, nor anyone who does what is detestable or false, but only those written in the Lamb's book of life.

♥ GOING DEEPER

1 Corinthians 15:42–49

[42] So it is with the resurrection of the dead: Sown in corruption, raised in incorruption; [43] sown in dishonor, raised in glory; sown in weakness, raised in power; [44] sown a natural body, raised a spiritual body. If there is a natural body, there is also a spiritual body. [45] So it is written, The first man Adam became a living being; the last Adam became a life-giving spirit. [46] However, the spiritual is not first, but the natural, then the spiritual.

[47] The first man was from the earth, a man of dust; the second man is from heaven. [48] Like the man of dust, so are those who are of the dust; like the man of heaven, so are those who are of heaven. [49] And just as we have borne the image of the man of dust, we will also bear the image of the man of heaven.

Colossians 3:1–4

THE LIFE OF THE NEW MAN

[1] So if you have been raised with Christ, seek the things above, where Christ is, seated at the right hand of God. [2] Set your minds on things above, not on earthly things. [3] For you died, and your life is hidden with Christ in God. [4] When Christ, who is your life, appears, then you also will appear with him in glory.

The New Jerusalem

Many Bible scholars have noted that Scripture is a journey from one garden to another—from the garden of Eden to the new Jerusalem, a garden city. Along the way, God placed markers pointing to the day when He will dwell with His people forever, sin and death defeated once and for all. Perhaps the most prominent of these markers is the

vision of a new temple He gave to the prophet Ezekiel. Accordingly, there are echoes of both the garden of Eden and Ezekiel's temple in the final chapters of Revelation.

Use this chart to fill in the corresponding descriptions of the new Jerusalem as you read Revelation 21–22.

THE GARDEN OF EDEN Genesis 2–3	EZEKIEL'S TEMPLE VISION Ezekiel 40–48	THE NEW JERUSALEM Revelation 21–22
Then the man and his wife heard the sound of the Lord God walking in the garden at the time of the evening breeze. GN 3:8	"…where I will dwell among the Israelites forever." EZK 43:7	RV 21:3
The Lord God said, "Since the man has become like one of us, knowing good and evil, he must not reach out, take from the tree of life, eat, and live forever." GN 3:22		RV 21:4

Continued

SHE READS TRUTH 103

THE GARDEN OF EDEN	EZEKIEL'S TEMPLE VISION	THE NEW JERUSALEM
Genesis 2–3	Ezekiel 40–48	Revelation 21–22
	In visions of God he took me to the land of Israel and set me down on a very high mountain. On its southern slope was a structure resembling a city.	
	EZK 40:2	RV 21:10
	…the glory of the Lord filled the temple.	
	EZK 43:5	RV 21:11, 23
	…the gates of the city being named for the tribes of Israel.	
	EZK 48:31	RV 21:12
	…saw a man…with a linen cord and a measuring rod in his hand.	
	EZK 40:3	RV 21:15

THE GARDEN OF EDEN	EZEKIEL'S TEMPLE VISION	THE NEW JERUSALEM
Genesis 2–3	Ezekiel 40–48	Revelation 21–22

Gold from that land is pure; bdellium and onyx are also there.		
GN 2:12		RV 21:18, 21
He drove the man out and stationed the cherubim and the flaming, whirling sword east of the garden of Eden to guard the way to the tree of life.		
GN 3:24		RV 21:25
A river went out from Eden to water the garden. From there it divided and became the source of four rivers.	…there was water flowing from under the threshold of the temple.	
GN 2:10	EZK 47:1	RV 22:1
The LORD God caused to grow out of the ground every tree pleasing in appearance and good for food, including the tree of life in the middle of the garden, as well as the tree of the knowledge of good and evil.	All kinds of trees providing food will grow along both banks of the river….Each month they will bear fresh fruit because the water comes from the sanctuary. Their fruit will be used for eating and their leaves for healing.	
GN 2:9	EZK 47:12	RV 22:2

The Source of Life

Revelation 22

THE SOURCE OF LIFE

¹ Then he showed me the river of the water of life, clear as crystal, flowing from the throne of God and of the Lamb ² down the middle of the city's main street. The tree of life was on each side of the river, bearing twelve kinds of fruit, producing its fruit every month. The leaves of the tree are for healing the nations, ³ and there will no longer be any curse. The throne of God and of the Lamb will be in the city, and his servants will worship him. ⁴ They will see his face, and his name will be on their foreheads. ⁵ Night will be no more; people will not need the light of a lamp or the light of the sun, because the Lord God will give them light, and they will reign forever and ever.

THE TIME IS NEAR

⁶ Then he said to me, "These words are faithful and true. The Lord, the God of the spirits of the prophets, has sent his angel to show his servants what must soon take place."

⁷ "Look, I am coming soon! Blessed is the one who keeps the words of the prophecy of this book."

⁸ I, John, am the one who heard and saw these things. When I heard and saw them, I fell down to worship at the feet of the angel who had shown them to me. ⁹ But he said to me,

"Don't do that! I am a fellow servant with you, your brothers the prophets, and those who keep the words of this book. Worship God!"

¹⁰ Then he said to me, "Don't seal up the words of the prophecy of this book, because the time is near. ¹¹ Let the unrighteous go on in unrighteousness, let the filthy still be filthy; let the righteous go on in righteousness; let the holy still be holy."

¹² "Look, I am coming soon, and my reward is with me to repay each person according to his work. ¹³ I am the Alpha and the Omega, the first and the last, the beginning and the end.

¹⁴ "Blessed are those who wash their robes, so that they may have the right to the tree of life and may enter the city by the gates. ¹⁵ Outside are the dogs, the sorcerers, the sexually immoral, the murderers, the idolaters, and everyone who loves and practices falsehood.

¹⁶ "I, Jesus, have sent my angel to attest these things to you for the churches. I am the root and descendant of David, the bright morning star."

¹⁷ Both the Spirit and the bride say, "Come!" Let anyone who hears, say, "Come!" Let the one who is thirsty come. Let the one who desires take the water of life freely.

¹⁸ I testify to everyone who hears the words of the prophecy of this book: If anyone adds to them, God will add to him the plagues that are written in this book. ¹⁹ And if anyone takes away from the words of the book of this prophecy, God will take away his share of the tree of life and the holy city, which are written about in this book.

²⁰ He who testifies about these things says, "Yes, I am coming soon."

Amen! Come, Lord Jesus!

²¹ The grace of the Lord Jesus be with everyone. Amen.

⬤ GOING DEEPER

Psalm 12:6

THE WORDS OF THE LORD ARE PURE WORDS, LIKE SILVER REFINED IN AN EARTHEN FURNACE, PURIFIED SEVEN TIMES.

Ezekiel 47:1–12

THE LIFE-GIVING RIVER

¹ Then he brought me back to the entrance of the temple and there was water flowing from under the threshold of the temple toward the east, for the temple faced east. The water was coming down from under the south side of the threshold of the temple, south of the altar. ² Next he brought me out by way of the north gate and led me around the outside to the outer gate that faced east; there the water was trickling from the south side. ³ As the man went out east with a measuring line in his hand, he measured off a third of a mile and led me through the water. It came up to my ankles. ⁴ Then he measured off a third of a mile and led me through the water. It came up to my knees. He measured off another third of a mile and led me through the water. It came up to my waist. ⁵ Again he measured off a third of

a mile, and it was a river that I could not cross on foot. For the water had risen; it was deep enough to swim in, a river that could not be crossed on foot.

⁶ He asked me, "Do you see this, son of man?" Then he led me back to the bank of the river. ⁷ When I had returned, I saw a very large number of trees along both sides of the riverbank. ⁸ He said to me, "This water flows out to the eastern region and goes down to the Arabah. When it enters the sea, the sea of foul water, the water of the sea becomes fresh. ⁹ Every kind of living creature that swarms will live wherever the river flows, and there will be a huge number of fish because this water goes there. Since the water will become fresh, there will be life everywhere the river goes. ¹⁰ Fishermen will stand beside it from En-gedi to En-eglaim. These will become places where nets are spread out to dry. Their fish will consist of many different kinds, like the fish of the Mediterranean Sea. ¹¹ Yet its swamps and marshes will not be healed; they will be left for salt. ¹² All kinds of trees providing food will grow along both banks of the river. Their leaves will not wither, and their fruit will not fail. Each month they will bear fresh fruit because the water comes from the sanctuary. Their fruit will be used for eating and their leaves for healing."

NOTES	Date

Genesis and Revelation

The books of Genesis and Revelation present a striking juxtaposition between the beginning and the end of time, revealing the ultimate redemption of humanity. This presents some of these parallels and their references.

Genesis

THE BEGINNING

In the beginning God… **GENESIS 1:1**

God created heaven and earth, eventually cursed by sin. **GENESIS 1:1**

Water symbolized unordered chaos. **GENESIS 1:2**

God created light and separated it from darkness. **GENESIS 1:3–5**

God gave humans dominion over the earth. **GENESIS 1:26–30**

God united Adam and Eve in marriage. **GENESIS 1:27–28; 2:18–25**

Satan introduced sin into the world. **GENESIS 3:1–7**

The serpent deceived humanity. **GENESIS 3:1–7, 13–15**

Sinful people refused to obey God. **GENESIS 3:3–6; 4:6–8**

Communion with God was forfeited. **GENESIS 3:8; 4:8**

God was abandoned by sinful people. **GENESIS 3:8–10**

Sinful people were ashamed to be in God's presence. **GENESIS 3:8–11**

People rebelled against the true God, resulting in physical and spiritual death. **GENESIS 3:8–19**

Sin brought pain. **GENESIS 3:16–17**

Sinful people were cursed. **GENESIS 3:16–19**

Sinful people were forbidden to eat from the tree of life. **GENESIS 3:22–24**

Sinful people were excluded from the bounty of Eden. **GENESIS 3:23**

Sinful people were sent away from the garden. **GENESIS 3:23–24**

Sinful people were banished from the presence of God. **GENESIS 3:24**

Sinful humanity was cursed with a wandering exile. **GENESIS 4:10–14**

Creation began to grow old and die. **GENESIS 5:3–31; 6:3**

Sin resulted in spiritual sickness. **GENESIS 6:5**

Water was used to destroy wicked humanity. **GENESIS 6–7**

Sinful people were scattered. **GENESIS 11:3–9**

Languages of sinful humanity were confused. **GENESIS 11:8–9**

"I am the Alpha and the Omega, the beginning and the end." **REVELATION 21:6**

God creates a new heaven and earth, where sin is nowhere to be found. **REVELATION 21:1**

There is no longer any sea. **REVELATION 21:1**

There is no more night or natural light; God Himself is the source of light. **REVELATION 21:23; 22:5**

God's people reign with Him forever. **REVELATION 20:4; 22:5**

God is united with his bride, the Church, in marriage. **REVELATION 19:7; 21:2, 9**

Satan and sin are judged. **REVELATION 19:11–21; 20:7–10**

The ancient serpent is bound to keep him from deceiving the nations. **REVELATION 20:2–3**

God's people worship Him. **REVELATION 22:3**

Genuine communion with God is experienced. **REVELATION 21:3, 7**

God's people (new Jerusalem, bride of Christ) are made ready for God and the marriage of the Lamb. **REVELATION 19:7–8; 21:2, 9–21**

God's people "see his face." **REVELATION 22:4**

God's people risk death to worship the true God and thus experience life. **REVELATION 20:4–6**

God comforts His people, removing death, grief, crying, and pain. **REVELATION 21:4**

The curse is removed from redeemed humanity. **REVELATION 22:3**

God's people may eat from the tree of life. **REVELATION 22:2, 14**

God's people are invited to the marriage feast of the Lamb. **REVELATION 19:9**

New Jerusalem includes a garden. **REVELATION 22:2**

God lives among His people. **REVELATION 21:3, 22; 22:4**

God's children are given a permanent home and an inheritance. **REVELATION 21:3–7**

Everything is made new. **REVELATION 21:5**

God heals the nations. **REVELATION 22:2**

God quenches thirst from the spring of life. **REVELATION 21:6; 22:1**

God's people unite to sing His praises. **REVELATION 19:6–8**

God's people are a multicultural people. **REVELATION 21:24, 26; 22:2**

THE END

Revelation

Take this day to catch up on your reading,
pray, and rest in the presence of the Lord.

ON THAT DAY IT WILL BE SAID,
"LOOK, THIS IS OUR GOD;
WE HAVE WAITED FOR HIM, AND HE HAS SAVED US.
THIS IS THE LORD; WE HAVE WAITED FOR HIM.
LET'S REJOICE AND BE GLAD IN HIS SALVATION."

Isaiah 25:9

Weekly Truth

Scripture is God breathed and true. When we memorize it, we carry the good news of Jesus with us wherever we go.

Throughout this plan, we have been memorizing verses that remind us of the holiness of God and call us to worship Him. This week, spend time memorizing Revelation 21:6.

THEN HE SAID TO ME, "IT IS DONE!
I AM THE ALPHA AND THE OMEGA,
THE BEGINNING AND THE END. I WILL
FREELY GIVE TO THE THIRSTY FROM THE
SPRING OF THE WATER OF LIFE."

Revelation 21:6

See tips for memorizing Scripture on page 120.

BENEDICTION

When he took the scroll, the four living creatures and the twenty-four elders fell down before the Lamb. Each one had a harp and golden bowls filled with incense, which are the prayers of the saints. And they sang a new song:

You are worthy to take the scroll and to open its seals,

because you were slaughtered,
and you purchased people
for God by your blood
from every tribe and language
and people and nation.
You made them a kingdom
and priests to our God,
and they will reign on the earth.

Then I looked and heard the voice of many angels around the throne, and also of the living creatures and of the elders. Their number was countless thousands, plus thousands of thousands. They said with a loud voice,

Worthy is the Lamb who was slaughtered

to receive power and riches
and wisdom and strength
and honor and glory and blessing!

I heard every creature in heaven, on earth, under the earth, on the sea, and everything in them say,

Blessing and honor and glory and power
be to the one seated on the throne,
and to the Lamb, forever and ever!

The four living creatures said, "Amen," and the elders fell down and worshiped.

REVELATION 5:8–14

RECOMMENDED READING

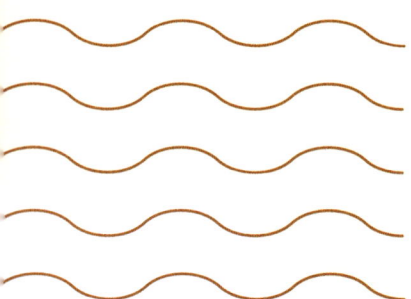

Attributes of God Daily Reading Guide

The Heart of Revelation
BY J. SCOTT DUVALL

Revelation for Everyone
BY N. T. WRIGHT

Tips for Memorizing Scripture

At She Reads Truth, we believe Scripture memorization is an important discipline in your walk with God. Committing God's Word to memory means we carry it with us and we can minister to others wherever we go. As you approach the Weekly Truth verses in this book, try these memorization tips to see which techniques work best for you!

STUDY IT

Study the passage in its biblical context, and ask yourself a few questions before you begin to memorize it: What does this passage say? What does it mean? How would I say this in my own words? What does it teach me about God? Understanding what the passage means helps you know why it is important to carry it with you wherever you go.

Break the passage into smaller sections, memorizing a phrase at a time.

PRAY IT

Use the passage you are memorizing as a prompt for prayer.

WRITE IT

Dedicate a notebook to Scripture memorization, and write the passage over and over again.

Diagram the passage after you write it out. Place a square around the verbs, underline the nouns, and circle any adjectives or adverbs. Say the passage aloud several times, emphasizing the verbs as you repeat it. Then do the same thing again with the nouns, then the adjectives and adverbs.

Write out the first letter of each word in the passage somewhere you can reference it throughout the week as you work on your memorization.

Use a whiteboard to write out the passage. Erase a few words at a time as you continue to repeat it aloud. Keep erasing parts of the passage until you have it all committed to memory.

CREATE

If you can, make up a tune for the passage to sing as you go about your day, or try singing it to the tune of a favorite song.

Sketch the passage, visualizing what each phrase would look like in the form of a picture. Or try using calligraphy or altering the style of your handwriting as you write it out.

Use hand signals or signs to come up with associations for each word or phrase, and repeat the movements as you practice.

SAY IT

Repeat the passage out loud to yourself as you are going through the rhythm of your day—getting ready, pouring your coffee, waiting in traffic, or making dinner.

Listen to the passage read aloud to you.

Record a voice memo on your phone, and listen to it throughout the day, or play it on an audio Bible.

SHARE IT

Memorize the passage with a friend, family member, or mentor. Spontaneously challenge each other to recite the passage, or pick a time to review your passage and practice saying it from memory together.

Send the passage as an encouraging text to a friend, testing yourself as you type to see how much you have memorized so far.

KEEP AT IT!

Set reminders on your phone to prompt you to practice your passage.

Purchase a She Reads Truth Scripture Card Set, or keep a stack of note cards with Scripture you are memorizing by your bed. Practice reciting what you've memorized previously before you go to sleep, ending with the passages you are currently learning. If you wake up in the middle of the night, review them again instead of grabbing your phone. Read them out loud before you get out of bed in the morning.

CSB BOOK ABBREVIATIONS

OLD TESTAMENT

GN Genesis	**JB** Job	**HAB** Habakkuk	**PHP** Philippians
EX Exodus	**PS** Psalms	**ZPH** Zephaniah	**COL** Colossians
LV Leviticus	**PR** Proverbs	**HG** Haggai	**1TH** 1 Thessalonians
NM Numbers	**EC** Ecclesiastes	**ZCH** Zechariah	**2TH** 2 Thessalonians
DT Deuteronomy	**SG** Song of Solomon	**MAL** Malachi	**1TM** 1 Timothy
JOS Joshua	**IS** Isaiah		**2TM** 2 Timothy
JDG Judges	**JR** Jeremiah	### NEW TESTAMENT	**TI** Titus
RU Ruth	**LM** Lamentations	**MT** Matthew	**PHM** Philemon
1SM 1 Samuel	**EZK** Ezekiel	**MK** Mark	**HEB** Hebrews
2SM 2 Samuel	**DN** Daniel	**LK** Luke	**JMS** James
1KG 1 Kings	**HS** Hosea	**JN** John	**1PT** 1 Peter
2KG 2 Kings	**JL** Joel	**AC** Acts	**2PT** 2 Peter
1CH 1 Chronicles	**AM** Amos	**RM** Romans	**1JN** 1 John
2CH 2 Chronicles	**OB** Obadiah	**1CO** 1 Corinthians	**2JN** 2 John
EZR Ezra	**JNH** Jonah	**2CO** 2 Corinthians	**3JN** 3 John
NEH Nehemiah	**MC** Micah	**GL** Galatians	**JD** Jude
EST Esther	**NAH** Nahum	**EPH** Ephesians	**RV** Revelation

BIBLIOGRAPHY

Barry, John D., David Bomar, Derek R. Brown, Rachel Klippenstein, Douglas Mangum, Carrie Sinclair Wolcott, Lazarus Wentz, Elliot Ritzema, and Wendy Widder, eds. *The Lexham Bible Dictionary.* Lexham Press, 2016.

Beale, G. K. *The Book of Revelation: A Commentary on the Greek Text.* Eerdmans, 2013.

Beale, G. K. *John's Use of the Old Testament in Revelation.* T&T Clark, 2015.

Beale, G. K. "Revelation." In *Commentary on the New Testament Use of the Old Testament.* Baker Academic, 2007.

Day, Colin. *Collins Thesaurus of the Bible.* Logos Bible Software, 2009.

Duvall, J. Scott. *Revelation.* Baker Books, 2017.

Duvall, J. Scott. *The Heart of Revelation.* Baker Books, 2016.

Duvall, J. Scott. *A Theology of Revelation.* Zondervan Academic, 2025.

ESV Study Bible: English Standard Version. Crossway, 2007.

Wright, N. T. *Revelation for Everyone.* Westminster John Knox Press, 2011.

FOR THE RECORD: REVELATION

You just spent 21 days in the Word of God!

MY FAVORITE DAY OF
THIS READING PLAN:

HOW DID I FIND DELIGHT IN GOD'S WORD?

ONE THING I LEARNED
ABOUT GOD:

WHAT WAS GOD DOING IN
MY LIFE DURING THIS STUDY?

WHAT DID I LEARN THAT I WANT TO SHARE
WITH SOMEONE ELSE?

A SPECIFIC PASSAGE OR VERSE
THAT ENCOURAGED ME:

A SPECIFIC PASSAGE OR VERSE THAT
CHALLENGED AND CONVICTED ME:

NOTES | Date